THE ACHIEVEMENTS OF
VATICAN II

IS VOLUME

1

OF THE

Twentieth Century Encyclopedia of Catholicism

UNDER SECTION

I

KNOWLEDGE AND FAITH

IT IS ALSO THE

141ST

VOLUME IN ORDER OF PUBLICATION

Edited by HENRI DANIEL-ROPS of the Académie Française

THE ACHIEVEMENTS
OF VATICAN II

By CHRISTOPHER HOLLIS

HAWTHORN BOOKS · PUBLISHERS · *New York*

#330145

First Edition, February, 1967

NIHIL OBSTAT

John A. Goodwine, J.C.D.
Censor Librorum

IMPRIMATUR

✠ Terence J. Cooke, D.D., V.G.

New York, New York DECEMBER 7, 1966

CONTENTS

CHAPTER I

THE CAUSE OF
THE COUNCIL

Many excellent books have been written about the Second
Vatican Council and the clash of personalities brought out
there. Xavier Rynne, Professor Novak, Mr Kaiser, Fr
Purdy and others are well known to all English readers
who are interested in the subject, and there are similar
books in other languages. Periodicals such as *Herder Correspondence, Concilium,* and regular papers such as *The
Tablet* have followed its course in detail. The actual text
of its decree is available. We do not wish to add to the
number of such books. This book is not concerned with a
description of personalities or to any large extent with a
description of how things happened. Its task is the rather
pedestrian one of summarizing what was decided at the
Council translated, as it were, into unofficial language. We
think that behind the generalities there is room for such
a work, for many have found it difficult to follow its unfamiliar proceedings, so different from those of a parliament or a congress.

After the First Vatican Council of 1870 there were
those who prophesied that since the pope's infallibility
had been defined, there would never again be a General
Council; they argued that the world no longer had any
need for one. The pope could now make decisions of his
own motion; when Pius XII defined the dogma of the As-

sumption in 1950, he did it *motu proprio* and with no consultation. But this interpretation derived from the impression that the definition of papal infallibility at the First Council was a total triumph for the Ultramontane school. There were many both inside and outside the Church who did at first think that the pope's power and authority were now unlimited. It was to combat the opinion of *The Times,* which thought that henceforth a Catholic would be obligated to defend the Massacre of St Bartholomew if the pope approved of it, that Newman and Manning had to write. Such a view was in fact based on a total misapprehension. The definition was by no means an unqualified victory for the Ultramontanes. "If I am obliged to bring religion into after-dinner toasts," wrote Newman to Gladstone, "I shall drink—to the pope if you please—still to conscience first and to the pope afterwards."

The formula that was eventually adopted was evolved by Cardinal Cullen, the Irish primate. The infallibility of the pope was very real but very exactly defined. His power was by no means the power of an absolute monarch who could impose his will upon the Church. It was rather a power to express under certain defined conditions the mind of the Church. In the years after 1870 the habit grew up of accepting without question every lightest word of the pope in a way that would never have been done in previous generations; that habit grew not at all out of the Vatican decrees but as a reaction of loyalty to Pius IX in face of the humiliations to which he was subjected by his imprisonment in the Vatican. That was not a time, loyal Catholics felt, in which it was decent to criticize the pope, even though he might not be speaking *ex cathedra.*

In fact, so far from the First Vatican Council having rendered any further Councils unnecessary, the Council was compelled by the Franco-Prussian War to break off with its labours uncompleted, and it was both necessary and inevitable, as Newman saw and wrote, that there should be another Council to carry those labours to completion. "The late definition," he wrote at the time of the First Council, "does not so much need to be undone as to be completed. It needs safeguards as to the pope's possible acts—explanations as to the matter and extent of his powers. Let us be patient, let us have faith and a new pope and reassembled Council may trim the boat." The First Vatican Council defined the position of the pope. Its agenda required that it go on to define the position of the bishops, the clergy and the laity—in fact the whole Church —but the war compelled its prorogation. It remained for its successors to complete its work.

Nevertheless, it must of course be admitted that, whatever the prophecies of Newman or the logic of the situation, no one had suggested summoning a new Council in all the years between the death of Pius IX in 1878 and the election of John XXIII; nor did anyone think when John was elected that that was to be the task he would set himself. It does not seem, as far as evidence shows us, that he had foreseen such a task for himself. There is some reason to think that the notion came to him by what, according to taste, we may call a sudden whim or the inspiration of the Holy Ghost and that John himself had not fully understood how such a Council would work or what would be the scope of its decisions or how long it would be likely to last.

It is the boast of the Church that its essential teachings are eternal. Nevertheless, it lives in the world. It is the Church of Him who was incarnated into the world, and its duty is to speak to the world; and the world changes its structure over the years and must therefore be spoken to in each age in a different language. It must avoid what Professor Novak has called "nonhistorical orthodoxy . . ." Nor has there ever been a period during which the structure of the Church has changed more rapidly than during the present century. Victory in the battle between Catholics and Protestants in the sixteenth and seventeenth centuries had really gone to the *tertius gaudens* of the secular State, and, in Catholic and in Protestant countries alike the status of the Church *vis-à-vis* the State was very different by the nineteenth century from what it had been in the Middle Ages. The nineteenth century was an age of secular progress, but that progress had entirely taken place in Protestant countries such as England and America. Yet the papacy of the nineteenth century had met the progress of the modern world only with resistance. The world, taught the early nineteenth-century popes, was a wicked and godless place. The Catholic must be prepared to retire before it into his catacombs and have as little to do with it as possible:

> *Hora novissima, tempora pessima*
> *Sunt. Vigilemus.*

In his *Syllabus Errororum*, which appeared in 1864, almost exactly a hundred years before the Second Vatican Council and in the same year as Newman's *Apologia*, Pius IX called down anathema on any who suggested that "the Roman pontiff" could accommodate himself to "liberty, progress or modern civilization."

This negative attitude was not ever the attitude taken by all Catholics. In France there was a sturdy band of liberal Catholics, such as Montalembert, Lacordaire and Lammenais, who, under the leadership of Bishop Dupanloup of Orleans, tried to wed the principles of the Revolution to the principles of the Church. "You made the Revolution," said Dupanloup, "without us and against us, yet for us, God willing it so in spite of you." These liberals did not meet with much favour at Rome. Lammenais' paper *L'Avenir* was condemned by Pope Gregory XVI in his *Mirari Vos* of 1832, and in his *Paroles d'un Croyant* Lammenais moved into assertions that were incompatible with any Catholic position. In Germany the great historian

Döllinger poured scorn on the claims of Italian scholarship and left the Church after the declaration of papal infallibility. But Montalembert, Lacordaire and Dupanloup remained Catholics, as did the English historian, Lord Acton, even though some of his books were put on the Index. There is no doubt that these men were wiser than the curial reactionaries of the day in seeing that the Church could not survive with a policy of mere antagonism to the whole progress of the modern world. If it found nothing to say to the problems facing the rising generation, the rising generation would leave it. The Church had to find some way of restating its eternal and unchangeable teachings in the language of the world of its day; and the man who above all showed it the way to do so was certainly John Henry Newman.

Newman had no illusions about the infidelity of his contemporaries and the likelihood that the next generation would be more unfaithful still. Yet in his *Essay on Development* he argued that the Christian revelation was not, as was at that time so commonly thought by both Catholics and Protestants, something that was delivered once and for all and that the faithful had only to preserve unchanged. On the contrary, Christ had left the Holy Spirit to direct the Church. Under the Spirit's direction the Church had the power to develop and define Christian teaching to meet the new challenges and conflicts of each passing age. This theory of development was, when first issued by Newman in 1846, a novelty to most Catholics and was by no means generally accepted. It met with much opposition. When in 1859 Newman followed it up with his article in the *Rambler* "On the Need for Consulting the Faithful in Matters of Doctrine," in which he argued that one could not always discover Catholic doctrine merely by appealing to the hierarchy, there was even more vigorous opposition. There had been, argued Newman, times—the Arian period in the fourth century or

England at the time of Henry VIII—when it was the bishops who had betrayed Catholic truth and the witness to it had been found elsewhere. But this essay had been delated to Rome by Bishop Brown of Newport, and for a time there was a distinct possibility that it would be put on the Index. As long as Pius IX was alive it could not be said that the voice of Newman or of any of the French liberals was in any way the voice of the Church. On the contrary, Cardinal Manning was in power in England, and the views that found favour in Catholic circles there were views of the most rigid Ultramontane variety.

It was only when Pius was succeeded by Leo XIII in 1878 that a wind of change blew through the Vatican. To Pius the Church had been a city under siege—a body on the defensive to be protected by proscription and censorship from the culture of an atheist world. To Leo, Christ had died for all men, and it was necessary, so far as it was possible, to tell his good news to all men. The faithful must indeed be protected, but preaching the Gospel to those who had not heard it was more important than protecting the faith of the faithful. In his *Rerum Novarum* Leo laid down the principles of a Catholic social teaching on the problems of the new industrialism. To show that he did not share his predecessor's suspicion of Newman, Leo made him a Cardinal. In the next reign, that of St Pius X, the papacy was involved in its controversy with modernism. Newman's line had been to accept the teaching of the Church but to suggest a method of argument by which that teaching could be convincingly defended. The modernists tried to change the Church's teaching to fit their interpretations. The two positions were radically different from one another. But some loose accusations were made both by modernists, who wanted to make their creed respectable, and by integralists, who wanted to throw suspicion on Newman by suggesting that the modernist theories derived from Newman's theory of development. The suggestion was specifically refuted by Pius X, who wrote to Bishop O'Dwyer of Limerick:

> Be assured that we strongly approve of your pamphlet proving that the works of Cardinal Newman, far from being at variance with our Encyclical are actually in close agreement with it. For even though in the works written before his conversion to the Catholic faith one might find statements which bear a certain likeness to some modernist formulas, you rightly deny that they in any way support them. . . . But as for the many and important books he composed as a Catholic, it is hardly necessary to repel the charges of affinity with the modernist heresy. . . . Indeed though things might be found which appear different from the ordinary theological mode of expression, nothing can be found which would arouse any suspicion of his faith . . . an excellent and most learned man. . . . You have done what you could among your own people and especially the English, to prevent those who have been abusing his name from deceiving the unlearned.

After the pope's words the suggestion that Newman was in any way tainted with modernism was clearly untenable. Yet perhaps the mere suggestion cast a certain temporary shadow over Newman's fame. However that may be, these shadows have passed and Newman's name remains. The developments of the modern world clearly require the Church to find some means of expressing itself in the modern idiom if its message is to remain at all relevant. John explicitly summoned the present Council not to define new doctrines but to give an *aggiornamento*—a bringing up to date—of the teaching of the Church—"to let fresh air into the Church," as he put it; and Cardinal Gracias of India explicitly announced to the Fathers that the spirit that presided over their deliberations was the spirit of Newman's theory of development. In the eulogy of Newman that Pope Paul VI incorporated into his address at the beatification of Blessed Dominic Barberi, he seemed to admit that Cardinal Gracias' claims were not exaggerated. "Newman's *Essay on the Development of Doctrine*," said Cardinal Gracias in the Council's debates on collegiality, "was the test by whereby the Council ought to be proved." Pope Paul spoke of Newman as "the promoter and representative of the Oxford Movement, which raised so many religious questions and excited such great spiritual energies; to him who in full consciousness of his mission—'I have work to do'—and guided solely by love of the truth and fidelity to Christ traced an itinerary the most toilsome but also the greatest, the most meaningful, the most conclusive, that human thought ever travelled during the last century, indeed one might say during the modern era, to arrive at the fullness of wisdom and of peace."

We can then fairly say that Newman saw more clearly than his contemporaries that if the Church was to survive in a developing world, it must have a formula of development that would allow it to adjust itself to a changing situation. The journalists who have attempted to draw a picture of dramatic contrast between Pius XII and John XXIII, as if one Government had fallen from office and had been succeeded by its opposition, have greatly exaggerated the story. Rome does not work like that. There were differences of personal temperament between Pius and John, but many of the policies that were carried nearer to fruition by his successor and by the Council were initiated by Pius XII. It was he who first set the machinery in motion for liturgical reform and for the renewal of biblical hermeneutics, and it was he who fought for world peace and for social reform. John XXIII most certainly never thought of himself as leading a reaction against Pius XII. He much more nearly thought of himself as following in Pius' footsteps. But, if we go back over a larger period, if we go back a hundred years, there has certainly been a great if gradual change in papal policy; and, insofar as he found an inspiration in the men of a hundred years ago, John found that inspiration far more in the progressive Catholics like Montalembert and Dupanloup and Newman, of whom Pius IX was so deeply suspicious, than he did in Pius or his entourage.

Whatever fine verbal distinctions we may draw, we cannot ignore the broad fact that John most fundamentally believed in freedom and in trusting people to be decent, and the early nineteenty-century popes most fundamentally had no such belief in any general human virtue. The world to John's predecessors was "on the wrong road"— a road that must inevitably lead to catastrophe and against which the pope must warn the people. Even Pius XII thought that "it is doubtful whether there has ever been an age like the present, an age in which men's spirits were so broken by despair, so busily alive to the difficulty of providing any remedy for their disorders." In his famous encyclical *Darkness Over the Earth* he drew a picture perhaps of some naiveté between the imagined concord of a united Christendom in medieval times and the present discords.

It is beyond question, he wrote, that, when the nations of Europe were still bound together by that common tie which observance of the same Christian law and tradition engenders, there were quarrels, there were revolutions, there were wars which brought havoc with them. But it is doubtful whether there has ever been an age like the present, an age in which men's spirits were so broken by despair, so busily alive to the difficulty of providing any remedy for their disorders. In earlier times men had a clear consciousness of what was right and what was wrong, what was allowable and what was forbidden. Such a consciousness made agreement easier, curbed the fierce appetites that had been aroused, opened and paved the way for an honourable settlement. In our day discords arise not merely from the violent impulses of an ungoverned temperament but more commonly from a confusion and a revolt in the depths of the human conscience. It is this which allows all the canons of private and public honesty and decency to be overthrown in our light-hearted modern fashion.

John, deep in his personal piety, had little feeling that the human race was divided into sheep and goats by religious denomination. He had also, like Teilhard de Chardin, an invincible optimism that the final purposes of God must be for good and that in the end, whatever the obstacles with which they might meet upon their way, those purposes would be achieved. It would be hard to imagine a more direct contrast to Pius XII's allocution than that of John XXIII's opening discourse to the Vatican Council:

> In the daily exercise of our pastoral office, we sometimes have to listen, much to our regret, to voices of persons who, though burning with zeal, are not endowed with much sense of discretion or measure. In these modern times they can see nothing but prevarication and ruin. They say that our era in comparison with past eras is getting worse. And they behave as though they had learned nothing from history, which is nonetheless the teacher of life, and as if at the times of other councils everything was full of triumph for the Christian ideas and for proper religious liberty. We feel that we must disagree with those prophets of doom, who are always forecasting disaster as though the end of the world were at hand. . . . Divine Providence is leading us to a new order of human relations which by men's own efforts, even beyond their very expectations, are directed towards the fulfilment of God's superior and inscrutable designs. Everything, even human differences, leads to the greater good of the Church.

Newman foresaw the necessity of a flexible policy that, to win a changing world, should be ready to find an answer to the new challenges. He did not foresee in detail all the problems of our world of today. How should he? For instance, the most clamorous demand of the modern world is that the Church should find a message for it on the problems of nuclear war and of birth control. The demand is reasonable, however difficult it may be to satisfy it. The Church has, of course, from her earliest years always seen war as a grave evil and laid down rigid conditions that must be satisfied before a war can be called a just war. Newman in his own day applied those tests to the Crimean War, then raging, and decided that it was not a just war. Benedict XV saw more clearly than any of the secular statesmen of the day the gigantic evil of the First World War and attempted—unfortunately without success—to bring it to an end. But neither Newman nor Benedict, of course, could have foreseen the peculiar moral problems set by the appalling new weapons, which are so destructive as to make it difficult to say that anyone who is using them is fighting a war of defence or that the consequences of them can be kept under control. And Newman, along with everybody else in the nineteenth century, was content to say that the use of methods for the prevention of birth was immoral. The modern casuistry arising out of the discovery of an allegedly safe period or the problems of the pill was of course unknown to him. Modern theologians are therefore called upon to give rulings on a number of particular problems with which he was not familiar. Although he did not foresee the details, such was of course exactly the sort of problem for which his theory of development was devised.

But the main change since Newman's day has been the decline of Europe and the expansion of the Church throughout the world. The Christian religion was not, of course, an intrinsically European affair. The Incarnation did not take place in Europe. The creeds were fashioned not by Europeans but by Asians and Africans. In its early centuries the Asian and African provinces of the Church were at least as vigorous as the European. It was only as a result of a great historical accident—one may say, of a great historical catastrophe—the destruction of the Asian and African provinces by the Mohammedan invasion—that Christendom was forced back into Europe as into a city under siege. Yet it was as such—as a body, Catholic and worldwide in its theoretical claims but in practice purely European in its government—that the Church lived for fourteen hundred years from the fifth century to the beginning of this century. When this century opened the Church was an entirely European body in its government. In the early years of the century Hilaire Belloc could write in his *Europe and the Faith,* "The Faith is Europe and Europe is the Faith." There were at the turn of the century only two cardinals who were not resident in Europe, and they—Cardinal Gibbons in America and Cardinal Moran in Australia—were both of European origins. Look around the world half a century later and how completely different a picture do we get! In secular affairs Europe, which had held the hegemony of the world since Homer's time, has lost it. In the last century all the Great Powers of the world were European Powers. Then Europe, which had entered the First World War as the possessor of all the Great Powers, emerged from the Second World War possessed of none. The two gigantic powers of Russia and the United States hung over the diminished Continent.

The Church had no reason to welcome the decline of Europe. In fact, during the 1914 war Benedict XV had, almost alone, warned the European Powers of their folly in destroying one another in their internecine war; but they paid no attention, and the Church had no alternative but to recognize the fact that Europe was no longer the mistress of the world. There has been a change in its organization as drastic as the change in the secular picture. We see today cardinals from Japan, China, Syria, India, Tanganyika, Mozambique, and the Philippines, who are not of

European origins, and at the same time a far higher representation from the peoples of European origins in North and South America. In the nineteenth century the normal Catholic was thought to live in a Catholic country in Western Europe. The desirable relation between Church and State was a relation of concordat by which the State recognized Catholicism as the national religion and accorded to the Church certain privileges. It was recognized that there were Catholics who did not live in such countries, who lived in non-Catholic countries in Europe such as Britain or who lived outside Europe altogether in countries whose tradition demanded a total separation of Church and State. There were Catholics not of European origins who lived in countries whose main tradition was not a Christian tradition at all. Such people must do the best they could—make what arrangements for toleration they could. But they were looked on by Rome as "external" members who could not expect to enjoy the full Catholic culture.

Today the position is totally reversed. In many European countries the concordats have collapsed. In such a country as France, for instance, the Church is no longer accorded any official status by the State; and, to most people's surprise, it has been found that in spite of the grave financial burdens the rupture of relations has brought with it and in spite of the immediately alarming decline in vocations, the Church has on the whole gained rather than lost from the breach. On the other hand, there has been a vast increase in the importance of the Catholics resident outside Europe—in the countries built on the tradition of a separation of Church and State—particularly in the United States. The result is that whereas in the nineteenth century the average Catholic lived in a Catholic country in Western Europe and the Catholic who did not live in such a country was the exception, today it is just the other way round. It is only in strange pockets of the world such as

Malta that Catholicism can in any way be called a State religion, practised by practically the whole population. The great majority of Catholics throughout the world live in countries where they have to live and work in the company of their non-Catholic fellow citizens.

When Pope John succeeded, he inherited problems created by the changing nature of the world. When he called for an *aggiornamento,* he was not wantonly inventing problems. A new world required new solutions. Pius XII, his predecessor, had recognized this as clearly as he, and under Pius XII non-Europeans had been introduced into the College of Cardinals. We had seen the beginnings of liturgical reforms, and in other ways the shape of things to come was beginning to show itself. What had not been suggested under Pius was that these reforms should be introduced by means of a Council. That was John's original contribution. How far John foresaw the detailed shape that the Council would take and how far he foresaw what its purpose would be, we cannot say. But it is certain that the main importance of the Council has lain not in its particular decisions but in its educative effect. Curial officials at Rome are probably neither more nor less regimented in their minds than officials anywhere else in the world. But the overcentralization at Rome, the necessity to refer there every trivial decision, was the cause of intolerable delays—for instance, in marriage cases—and it was an abuse that decisions about the affairs of people of every culture and in every quarter of the world should be entirely in the hands of Italians. Nor, although one need not accept every sweeping accusation, could it be pretended that the relations of curial officials with the Fascist régime or its later interventions in Italian politics were such as to make it possible for one to leave in their hands with an easy mind the entire control of the Church.

It is in the nature of the bureaucratic mind that it tends to think that it possesses a certain mystique—that things

can be done only the way it does them—and that any
changes in method must necessarily lead to catastrophe.
Naturally, this conservative mentality was often found
among the curial officials, and if a new situation required
new policies, any pope who attempted to introduce reforms by whatever method would almost certainly meet
with some opposition. Pius XII had spoken of reforming
the curia and had drafted legislation for that purpose. But
he never got so far as to enact it. His method of meeting
the opposition was to confront it with ruthless and energetic autocracy. He took more power into his own hands
than had any of his predecessors. He made access to himself difficult. He acted for years as his own Secretary of
State. John, the jovial, approachable easy-mixer, was a
very different sort of man. He had the talent such as few
have had of breaking a sound barrier. He made himself
loved by men and women in all parts of the world of every
kind and creed as perhaps no other pope in history has
ever done; and when reforms were necessary, he preferred that they should be voluntarily accepted rather
than imposed by authority. So he determined to summon a
General Council. John differed greatly from his predecessors in that he had spent his life much more in the company of men of the world and much less in Vatican corri-
dors than had other popes. It may be that, as a result, he
was more aware of what the world was thinking and saying than they had been. Anyway, what the event proved
was that bishops in various parts of the world had come
very strongly to feel the need of a reform of the Church, but
they lived in such isolation from one another that each
bishop thought that he was largely unique in his progressive ideas and was prepared to believe that the general
mind of the Church was so overwhelmingly opposed to
such changes that it was useless to demand them. The
bishops, congregating at Rome, discovered to their amaze-
ment that although each had thought previously that he

held a solitary opinion, in fact they very largely agreed with one another, and throughout the Council progressive motions were always carried by overwhelming majorities.

CHAPTER II

THE FIRST SESSION

The first session of the Second Vatican Council was inaugurated by John XXIII on October 2nd, 1962. At the First Vatican Council the seven hundred and forty-four bishops who attended could easily be accommodated in a transept of St Peter's. To this Second Council came 2,540 bishops from every corner of the world. Little more than a third of them were from European sees. In his address Pope John rebuked "the prophets of doom" who were for ever proclaiming the imminent catastrophe of the world. The days of the State Church were over, and it was very doubtful what advantage on balance the Church had derived in the past from the support of the State. "The princes of this world," he said, "sometimes in all sincerity intended thus to protect the Church, but more frequently this occurred not without spiritual damage and danger." In the age that was coming to birth the Church must not seek to maintain its authority by the weapons of repression. It must "rule with the medicine of mercy rather than with severity." Other councils had been called to define new doctrines. But the purpose of this Council was to enable the Church "to bring herself up to date" and thus to bring nearer the time of the reunion of Christendom, when Christ's prayer "that they may be all one" should be fulfilled.

These were brave words, and when that evening the pope, in the true spirit of a father, showed himself on the balcony of the Vatican and gave his blessing to the crowds

in the piazza below him, bidding them go home and give a
kiss to their children and an extra one from the pope, the
hardest and most cynical could not fail to be moved. But,
of course, as everybody knows, it is often all too easy to
manage a popular assembly and to prevent it from giving
free expression to its opinions. In every country today
there are complaints, justified or unjustified, about the excessive control over legislative assemblies of party ma-
chines. Summoning the bishops from America and Asia
and Africa to help to free the Church from an excessive
curial domination, Pope John had indeed, more truly
than Canning, called the new world in to redress the balance of the old, but it was not yet certain that his invitation would be successful. There are two sorts of council or
assembly in the religious as in the secular world. There is
the genuinely free council, where members express their
uninhibited opinions and reach genuine conclusions.
There are councils where the real decisions have all been
made beforehand by the managers and where the council
gives no more than a formal and automatic approval to
decisions that have already been made elsewhere. There
had been all too many accusations, sustained or not, of
improper pressure brought to bear at the First Vatican
Council. The first task of the Fathers at this Second Council was to show whether this Council should be of that sort
or not—whether it should be a free or a tied council.

It was notorious that there were curial officials who
were by no means pleased that the pope had summoned a
general council at all, who would gladly have stopped it if
they could, and who, when that proved impossible, wished
that at least nothing much should come of it. They thought
that things were very well as they were—or at any rate
that they were much more likely to be made worse than
to be made better. They hoped, like Evelyn Waugh, for
"the mixture as before." When they found that they could
not prevent it, the curial critics set themselves to manage it.

They saw to it that nearly every preparatory commission, which was to prepare the schemata for the Council's consideration, was headed by a curial cardinal. They hoped in this way to control the agenda the Council was to consider. They had prepared a list of the bishops who were to serve on the various commissions, and they planned to present these lists to the plenary session of the Council in the hope that the Council would give their lists an automatic and unanimous acceptance. It did not turn out like that. At the Council's first meeting, when the lists were submitted, Cardinal Liénart of Lille and Cardinal Frings of Cologne protested against such a procedure. The bishops, they argued, had not yet had an opportunity to make proper inquiries among their brethren. It was absurd that they should be asked to make their decisions in this fashion. Cardinal Liénart moved the adjournment of the Council to meet again some days later when the bishops had had an opportunity to make proper inquiries. This motion was unanimously accepted, and twenty minutes after their first meeting the bishops were out in St Peter's Piazza. It was the first and most significant of victories— the sign that the bishops refused to be railroaded or used as rubber stamps.

There is, of course, a price to be paid for free debate. The argument that is always advanced in favour of some sort of party organization in a council or an assembly or a parliament is that without it nothing would ever get done, and there is, of course, a great deal of truth in such an argument. John doubtless knew this as well as anyone else or at least would very soon have come to understand it. With two and a half thousand bishops attending, debates would be interminably prolonged if every bishop were allowed to speak on whatever subject and at whatever length he wished. There would be unendurable repetition. If business was to be accomplished, there would have to be rules of procedure and some regulation of debate. But it was important that these rules should be rules that the Fathers imposed on themselves after they had learned from experience that they needed them and not rules imposed on them from on high or by curial edicts. It was inevitable, therefore, that the debates of the first session should be somewhat incoherent and inconclusive and that there should not be much in the way of definitive achievement until the Fathers had learned how to regulate their own business. There was no harm in this even though the impatient might complain of it. For the preliminary debates, although they led to no definite decisions, gave the Fathers the opportunity to get to know one another and to adjust their minds to the problems that were presented to them, many of which were quite unfamiliar to many of them. Had decisions been made rapidly, they must necessarily have been decisions of the mere acceptance of official opinion, which was just what Pope John most wished to avoid.

The first months were mainly occupied with the work of the commissions that were preparing the documents for subsequent submission to the full Council. On its assembly the Council was faced with a vast compendium of some seventy documents on various matters of doctrine and discipline. It was obvious that, if any such volume of schemata were to be issued, the public throughout the world would be confused and bewildered, would lose interest in the Council's deliberations; it would thus fail in its main purpose of persuading the world of the relevance to its problems of the Church's teaching. The first task then was simply to coordinate these drafts and reduce them to fewer headings. The task was primarily a technical one, but it gave birth to certain controversies. Controversy was particularly keen over the first suggested draft of the constitution of the schema on Revelation, one of the first to be submitted to the Council. The issues were whether the doctrine of Revelation should be expressed in the old-fashioned scholastic language or whether the opportunity should be taken to recast it in language less technical and more easily intelligible to the ordinary modern man, and in particular whether it was to be stated that Revelation was expressed only in Tradition or in Tradition and the Scriptures. As the Church admitted the authority of the Scriptures and as it was the Tradition of the Church that decided which books were to be admitted into the canon of the Scriptures, it might seem at first that the controversy was not of major importance, just as the terminology in which its conclusions were expressed might seem to be a secondary matter. But, of course, if the prime purpose of the Council was to make the Church's teaching as easily comprehensible to the world as possible, the manner of its expression was of importance.

In his condemnation of modernism in his encyclical *Pascendi Gregis,* St Pius X had insisted that all Catholic teaching should be in the scholastic language; and while the revival of neo-Thomism was wholly to be welcomed, there could be no doubt that the insistence on the discussion of these problems exclusively in Thomistic phrases when the world at large was discussing them in other phrases had set up an unnecessary barrier between Catholic philosophers and those of the world at large. On the question of Scripture, as is known, it was—and indeed still is—the complaint of Protestants against the Church that Catholics accept certain doctrines that have no Scriptural warrant. The Protestants claimed that they were appealing back to the pure teaching of Christ and the Scriptures against later sacerdotal corruptions. If it had really been Catholic teaching to disregard the evidence of Scripture, this would of course have been a matter upon which it would have been immoral to pretend agreement; but since Catholic doctrine admits the authority of Scripture, there could be little purpose in causing an unnecessary obstacle by refusing to say so. Catholics, of course, have

never admitted that Catholic beliefs were invented subsequently to the Scriptures. According to Catholic belief
the Church teaches with its own authority. Nevertheless,
there are to be found in the Bible suggestions, at least,
of Catholic doctrines, even if in some cases further definition was needed to make the doctrine exact. It was therefore possible to say that the Church's doctrine derives
from Tradition and Scripture. Neither statement was exactly inaccurate. On the other hand, to omit all mention
of the authority of Scripture would clearly appear to be an
aggressive challenge to the Protestant reader; and since
one of the main objects of the Council was the ecumenical
object, the desire to bring nearer the day of reunion between the different denominations, omission of all mention of Scripture was unfortunate. There was, therefore,
vigorous objection to the original draft that was presented
to the Fathers, which was guilty of this omission. On a
vote taken on November 20th, 1962, 1,368 voted in favour of the draft being returned and rewritten. 812 were
in favour of accepting it.

The trouble was that according to the strict rules of procedure of the Council a majority of two to one was required for the rejection of a document. The votes were
therefore not sufficient for such a rejection in the formal
sense. On the other hand, it was clearly impossible to put
out as the pronouncement of the Council a document
that had been so heavily defeated on the vote. An impasse
seemed to have been reached—an impasse that could be
resolved only by the personal intervention of the pope. It
was the first time that Pope John was called upon to show
his hand on a matter that had aroused controversy within
the Council, and how he did so showed clearly where his
own sympathies lay. Of his own motion he withdrew
the document and set up a mixed commission consisting
of members of the Theological Commission, of the Secretariat of Unity, and a few other specially appointed Car-

dinals to draw up a new document. Conservative theologians had until then taken the position that it was their
business to state the doctrine of the Church and that the
Secretariat of Unity had the right to carry on such negotiations as might be possible with other denominations
on the basis of the doctrine the theologians provided for
them. They had no right to help draw up those doctrines
themselves. The pope's decision was of great importance
as the first assertion of a right of the Secretariat to sit in on
the drafting of such documents. The decision of the majority of the Council and of the pope insisted that it was
the duty of the Secretariat of Unity not only to negotiate
on accepted doctrine but also to make "a new effort to
bring Christian doctrine home."

The meaning of the word "ecumenical," so often attached to the Council, was not then, and indeed is not
even now, quite clear. "Ecumenical" means "of the inhab-
ited world." Was this to be a Council of representatives
from the different denominations of the world to see if
they could compose their differences, much as the Council of Florence in 1438 was a meeting between Roman
and Greek ecclesiastics to try to compose the differences
between their two Churches? Or was it to be a meeting
only of Catholics from all the countries of the world to settle what should be the teaching and policy of the Catholic
Church? Pope John's formation of the Secretariat of Christian Unity under Cardinal Bea in 1961 had shown how
deeply he responded to our Lord's prayer that his disciples might be "all one," and of course the Council has
led to a great and welcome relaxation of the disciplinary
rules that govern joint meetings of Catholics and non-
Catholics. Observers from the other denominations were
invited, and, with the exception of the Greek Orthodox,
came to the Council. They were welcomed and treated
with courtesy, and few would deny that as a result of the
activities of the Council, the relations between Christians

of the different denominations are today more friendly than they have ever been in history. Nevertheless, the Council has been in its membership a Council of Catholics for the *aggiornamento* of the Catholic Church.

The most important immediate contribution to unity of the Catholic Church has been, it has been judged, its attempt to set its own house in order—not to pretend that it can abandon essential positions but to see to it that it remedies its own defects and removes unnecessary obstacles that may have arisen out of offensive habits of expression. It was with such an intention that the Council considered the schema on Mass Communications Media. The ecclesiastical tradition had been one of considerable hostility to the press. The early nineteenth-century popes had been all too ready, like Gregory XVI, to denounce the notion of the freedom of the press as "a madness," and it was almost taken for granted that journalists, if they wrote about the Church at all, would be certain to write about it unfavourably. It was a part of the siege mentality of those earlier days that Catholics should have as little to do with journalists as possible. The First Vatican Council offered no facilities for the press at all. When the Second Council began, the journalists still found much to complain of, and facilities were certainly markedly inferior to those they would have expected to receive at any secular conference. Yet those among them who had some historical knowledge were perhaps able to understand that if Roman officials were doing less than they might have done, they were still doing a great deal more than had ever been done by any of their predecessors. And, although the document itself was not very inspiring in either its first draft or its final form, it was perhaps valuable as an evidence of a willingness to accept the spirit of *aggiornamento* that the Council thought it desirable to include a schema on Mass Communications Media among its documents. The reason it was this schema alone whose draft received approval at this first session was that it was comparatively innocuous and uncontroversial. So it was passed, perhaps because of the feeling that even at this first session something should be passed in order to allay the criticism of those who were inclined to argue, owing to their lack of understanding of the need for preliminary work in the commissions, that the Council did not seem to be achieving anything. Yet it is by now generally agreed that this schema was both the least important and the least worthy of the Council's schemata. It is perhaps unfortunate that it should in this way have won pride of place.

The argument whether tradition alone or Tradition and Scripture were the sources of Revelation did not greatly excite the ordinary man in the street, and the schema on Mass Media did not seem to have anything to say that was especially surprising. All the interest that was aroused in the first session was aroused by the suggestions for liturgical reform. They alone seemed to be likely to touch the lives of the ordinary Catholic. Liturgical reform was, of course, in no way an invention of the Council. Over the years the active participation of the laity in the services of the Church had been reduced to a minimum. The common use of the word "hearing" Mass in place of "assisting at" Mass bears witness to it, and the turbulence of much popular Protestant disorder at the time of the Reformation led the Council of Trent to welcome a situation in which the mysteries were celebrated by the priest at the altar and the laity took no active part in the service. The Western Church, alone among all religious bodies, Christian or non-Christian, had in its early years developed the habit of celebrating its mysteries not as others did, in secret or behind a screen, but in the full view of the congregation. The move toward a more secret Mass was a move away from the original Western tradition. The reaction against it was a reaction to an original form, not a revolutionary novelty.

In the early years of this century the reaction against it had already begun to show itself. At the height of his campaign against modernism St Pius X, the least revolutionary of men, had urged the faithful to take the sacraments more frequently than had been customary in the immediately preceding years. Pius XII was keenly interested in liturgical reform. He allowed evening Mass, liberalized the rules about fasting, and reformed the Holy Week liturgy. More important perhaps, in these years there began to spring up in many countries—particularly in Germany —what was then the new custom of dialogue Mass. This required no explicit papal or episcopal permission. There was never any rule of the Church ordaining that the responses in Mass should be made only by the server—that the congregation should remain silent.

It was again logically required by the development of events that the vernacular should play a larger part in the Mass. Latin was in no way the uniquely Christian language. The Eucharist was not instituted in Latin, and Greek, not Latin, was the language of the Church in its early centuries. The Church only adopted Latin in the Western world because Latin—in many ways a somewhat rude and very unclassical Latin—was the vernacular of the Christian world after Christendom had been robbed by Mohammedan conquest of its Asian and African provinces. Throughout the Middle Ages and until modern times all educated people in Western Europe learned Latin as a part of their education. The Protestant revolt against the Church had been in most countries a largely nationalist revolt—Englishmen and Germans objected to being ruled by Italians and Frenchmen. Yet all the Catholic countries, with the exceptions of Ireland and Poland, were countries that had formed a part of the Roman Empire. They spoke languages that derived from Latin. It was reasonable to ask them to pray in Latin as a symbol of the supranational nature of the Church.

In this century, when the Church was no longer a pre-dominantly European body, the situation was quite different. American Catholics, of course, derived from one or other of the European nations, but, since it was only their ancestors who had lived in the country of Roman tradition, their links with Latin, though not nugatory, were more tenuous than those of the Catholics in Europe. Indeed, the Irish-American Catholics—and there were a great many of them—came from the one country of Western Europe that had never been a part of the Roman Empire, that had no Roman architectural monuments, and whose connection with Latin was therefore more slender than that of other Catholic countries. Therefore, once the shock to the natural conservatism of American opinion was overcome and the American Catholic realized that the matter was, so to speak, negotiable, Americans were generally in favour of liturgical reform. But apart from the Americans there were, of course, the Catholics from Asian and African countries that had never known anything of the Roman tradition and whose languages were quite unconnected with Latin. Such Catholics—such as they were—had not previously been much considered in the organization of the Church. Catholicism was considered to be a Latin business, and it was a part of their conversion that they should, as far as they could, accept the Latin culture as well as the Catholic religion. The situation in our day, with European rule over the Asian and African continents in collapse, is wholly different. To the Catholics in such countries Latin, far from being a symbol of unity with their coreligionists, has become a reminder of that imperialism against which on the political plane they have been so strongly fighting. It seemed to carry with it a suggestion that Catholicism was an especially European religion.

There were, of course, plenty of problems of detail still to be settled—there are indeed plenty of problems of detail still to be settled even now. If the vernacular was to be introduced into the Mass, it was clearly essential that the new versions should be entirely worthy versions. Such versions could not easily be written overnight. In every country there are still arguments going on about this or that phrase of the new versions. No wise man wishes Latin to be entirely and under all circumstances discarded from the services of the Church. Its tradition is too great for it to be thus wholly forgotten. After all, "it has fought and conquered the centuries" as no other language has. Pope John himself had paid his tribute to it in *Veterum Sapientia*. It is reasonable that it should be used in public before congregations of mixed nationalities and that elderly priests who have been saying Mass in Latin for many years should be allowed to continue to do so.

All these problems remained to be settled at the end of the first session, and to a large extent still remain to be settled. All that the first session of the Council did was to accept in principle that the use of the vernacular in the Mass was permissible and to instruct the various national hierarchies to prepare detailed schemes for their countries. It was important at this stage primarily as evidence that some definite change that would effect the lives of every ordinary Catholic would certainly come out of the Council; but it was a curiosity that the one definite change of the one session for which Pope John was spared should be a change to which John was not himself especially sympathetic. For, like so many Italian ecclesiastics, John was a great lover of Latin and appeared to have shown in his *Veterum Sapientia* that his own sympathies were opposed to any weakening of the Latin tradition in the Church.

At the end of the first session Pope John announced that the preliminary schemata that had been drawn up by Cardinal Ottàviani should be set aside and that new ones for final ratification in the second session should be worked out by a new commission consisting of "several cardinals and bishops" under the chairmanship of Cardinal Cicognani, the Vatican Secretary of State. It was a proof that the Council was to be allowed to go forward to a genuine *aggiornamento* of the Church and that John would not be content with any half measures of merely verbal reform. On December 8th, 1962, he delivered his closing address to the first session.

> The first session was like a slow and solemn introduction to the great work of the Council—a generous willingness to enter into the heart and substance of our Lord's plan. It was necessary for brothers, gathered together from afar around a common hearth to make each other's closer acquaintance; it was necessary for them to look at each other squarely in order to understand each other's hearts; they had necessarily to describe their own experiences, reflecting the conditions of the apostolate under the most varied climates and circumstances, in order that there should be a thoughtful and profitable interchange of views on personal matters.

It was clear from his words that the pope was determined that the Council should go forward, but there were already disturbing rumours about his health, and as the Fathers dispersed, none could feel confident that John would be there to preside over them when they met again.

CHAPTER III

THE SECOND SESSION

The Council, of course, was not to see Pope John again. As all the world knows, he died on June 3rd, 1963, mourned and loved as hardly any pope in history had ever been. Cardinal Montini, Archbishop of Milan, was elected to succeed him after one of the shortest consistories on record, and he took the title of Paul VI. The change involved a certain reorganization, but the new pope took the first opportunity to announce that he would continue the Council of his predecessor and that in spite of all this work of reorganization its second session should be postponed only a few weeks from the date originally set by Pope John. It was to meet on September 29th, just three weeks later than the original date.

The second session—the session of the autumn of 1963—ended in something of a disappointment. If it was one of the purposes of the Council, as John had proclaimed, to further the unity of all Christians, then it was clearly the duty of the Council not only to reaffirm whenever necessary the fundamental teachings of the Church but at the same time to dissociate the Church from any incidental and unessential positions into which it may have drifted through the accidents of former times. We have already seen the anxiety of the Fathers to make it clear that in Catholic teaching Scripture was one of the sources of Revelation. In a similar spirit it was desirable, because of the susceptibilities of both non-Catholics and Catholics outside Western Europe, to make it clear that it was not Catholic policy to demand any State's support of the Church or a privileged position for the Church before secular law and that the maxim of *Extra Ecclesiam nulla salus* did not mean that Catholics denied all virtue or all hope of salvation to those who were not members of the visible Catholic Church here on earth. From this point of view the most important of the schemata of the Council were those on religious liberty, in which the Council proclaimed unequivocally the right and duty of all men to proclaim and practise the religion their consciences led them sincerely to embrace, and on ecumenism, which defined the relationship between the Catholic Church and other religious bodies.

It was perhaps a pity that it should have taken so long before the Council could carry to a conclusion its deliberations on those schemata, but wise men understood that if the Council was to continue as a free Council, it was inevitable that it should advance somewhat slowly. In particular, it was to no purpose to define the relationship of the Catholic Church with other bodies or the rights of those outside the Church until the Council had first decided what the Church was. The first and fundamental schema to be considered was necessarily that on the nature of the Church.

This necessity was from the first apparent to Pope Paul's ordered mind. There were some who argued that Pope John was indeed the man with his enthusiasms and his lovable personality to launch such a Council. There were many who wished well to the Council only because it was the child of Pope John's enthusiasm. This was an important advantage, but, it was said, there was little reason to think that he had the gifts of a chairman of committee, and Pope Paul would be better able to carry business through. Whether John would or would not have proved capable of this business in committee, we shall never know. As for Pope Paul, it may well prove in the end to be the verdict of history that he was a man of great capacity, but of course it was by no means proved that he was able to carry through his business easily, even if in the end he carried it through successfully. Successful management was not particularly evident in the second session. Before the beginning of the session the new pope announced the appointment of four moderators—Cardinal Döpfner of Munich, Cardinal Suenens of Brussels, Cardinal Agagianian and Cardinal Lercaro of Bologna—to direct the proceedings on the floor of the Council. The three who had dioceses were all strong progressives by reputation, and it was thought that their appointment would be a guarantee that integralist opinion would not at any point frustrate the purposes of the majority of the Fathers.

At the same time the pope announced new rules of procedure. Fifty bishops could sign a new document and demand its transmission to the coordinating commission. If five members of a commission desired a secret vote, it must be granted. To close discussion on a point only a simple majority was required. A two-thirds majority was required to approve a document. A bishop who wished to speak after the closure had been invoked could do so if he got the support of five signatures. The pope announced his intention of reforming the curia so as to give it a "larger supernational vision" and to have it "educated with a more accurate ecumenical preparation." He extended his welcome to the observers from other denominations. All these gestures showed the pope's determination that the Council should be a free Council and his sympathy with progressive opinion; but, of course, it was certain to prove true, as Pope John had discovered, that there were difficulties in allowing too great freedom to a very large assembly. The difficulty was, as has been said, the purely practical one that without firm rules of procedure nothing would ever get done. Also, if unlimited freedom was

allowed to minorities, though such concessions might be
intended to favour the progressives, they could very easily be used by the opponents of the progressives, who
were primarily anxious to see to it that nothing got done.

So the measures by which it was hoped that the moderators would have firm control over the debates were by no
means entirely successful. Tension arose between some
of the commissions and the General Assembly. A general vote of the Assembly demanded the inclusion of a
recognition of the collegial nature of the episcopacy in
the schema of the Church. Cardinal Döpfner as modera-
tor ruled that this instruction was binding on the Theological Commission, which was preparing the schema. Cardinal Ottaviani, its president, and Cardinal Browne, its
vice president, refused to accept it as binding. The pope
attempted to break the impasse by adding to the Theological Commission five additional members, all of whom
had been strong supporters of the majority view in the
Assembly, thus bringing the opinion of the majority of
the Theological Commission into line with the opinion of
the General Assembly.

There was no drastic change in the number of bishops
who attended the second session from that at the first.
Throughout both sessions it ran steadily at something
about 2,200 or 2,300 a meeting out of the 3,000 odd bishops in the world. On the other hand, as the commissions
got down to work, there was a very steep increase in the
number of *periti,* or theological experts, which rose from
185 to 383. The first session had been almost entirely
concerned with a work of prevention; the bishops tried to
stake a claim to real independence and firmly asserted
their determination to see that the Council was not stage-
managed by curial officials, that it was not treated as a
mere continuation of the First Vatican Council, and that
it was not compelled to express its conclusions merely in
pious scholastic generalizations that would make little

impact on the modern world, which was unacquainted with such methods of expression. With the second session the Council attempted to get down to real work. Yet the work was naturally not accomplished without its difficulties.

The conservatives among the bishops—whether members of the curia or not—had at first made no bones about the fact that they hoped that nothing very drastic would come out of the Council; at first they pinned their hopes on the curial officials, thinking that they with their superior knowledge of organization would be able to manage the business satisfactorily. When that proved not to be so easy owing to the assertion by the progressives of their right to due membership of the commissions, their opponents organized themselves into what was almost a definite conservative party in the Assembly. They could only command a very small minority of the bishops, and whenever it came to a straightforward vote, they were always defeated by some ten to one; but they were fertile in devising procedural delays and hardly concealed their hope that if they spun out the proceedings long enough, the Fathers might wish to slip off home or to agree that anything or nothing should be done in order to bring the wearisome proceedings to an end. Although the pope had made it fairly clear that his own sympathies were on the whole with the progressives, he was desperately anxious to avoid any cleavage in the Church. He did not wish to see one opinion, even if it was that of a strong majority, riding roughshod over another and was determined that, wherever possible, unanimity should reign. This meant that an obstinate minority had considerable opportunity to push its views.

The first two issues that were to be considered at this session were those of the dogmatic constitution of the Church and the cognate question of the pastoral office of the bishops. It had never been the intention of the First

Vatican Council to suggest that the pope alone in the Church had authority. That only the authority of the pope was exactly defined by the Council was, as has been said, simply because of the accident that the Franco-Prussian War dissolved the Council before the later items in its agenda were reached. The developments of the world between 1870 and 1963 added powerful pragmatic reasons to the reasons of theology for a proper definition of the functions of members of the Church other than the pope. The case for a measure of decentralization in the Church's administration was overwhelming. The delays in getting routine decisions from Rome were notorious and scandalous. Yet, although obstinate conservatism played its part, it was not merely obstinate conservatism that insisted that there were two sides to this controversy. Progressives are often not very good at seeing the dangers of the policies they are advocating. They think their case is more completely self evident than it is. Even if it was admitted that decentralization was necessary, it was by no means obvious to whom authority should be delegated.

Christ gave authority to bishops as clearly as he gave it to St Peter. That was to be admitted. Establishing the apostles, he established a college of bishops. "The decisive point in the document on the Church," wrote Karl Rahner, "is the description of the function of the entire episcopate as a body—the college of bishops—as a body, not as individual bishops nor even as a sum of individuals." So much must be granted, but some bishops were inclined almost to take it for granted that if authority was to be decentralized, then it should be vested in national episcopal councils. But although there is abundant evidence that Christ gave authority to bishops and that the first bishops—the apostles—operated as a company or, if you will, as a college, there is no evidence at all that he gave authority to national episcopacies. There remained, therefore, a question on which we had no revealed guid-

ance. Should authority be vested in the individual diocesans, or should it be given to national episcopacies? Some
people took it almost for granted that the latter should be
the policy, but it was a policy that carried with it almost
as many dangers as it could pretend to remedy. Some
countries, such as England and Ireland, had for many
years held national episcopal conferences. Other countries had no such custom. There is clearly no reason why
such conferences should not be held if they are a convenience, but should they be given any jurisdictional
power? There was acute difference in particular among
the American cardinals about such conferences and their
status. Cardinal Ritter thought such conferences "necessary for an effective ministry today." Cardinal Meyer was
sceptical. Cardinal McIntyre and Cardinal Spellman were
opposed. "National episcopal conferences," thought Cardinal McIntyre, "can be accepted if they are on a volun-
tary basis but are to be deplored if they assume a strictly
juridical character." "The pope had full power over the
entire Church," thought Cardinal Spellman. "He does
not need the help of others."

In the conflict of Protestants and Catholics during the
sixteenth and seventeenth centuries victory had, as has
been said, gone not to the Protestants or to the Catholics
but to the secular national States. The greatest danger to
the Church in the eighteenth century had come from the
attacks of the Gallicanism and Josephism of the philo-
sophical monarchs of the day. The exaltation of the papacy
in the nineteenth century had been a reaction against that
evil, and though it may well be that it carried with it its
own dangers, yet it had not in itself been an unnecessary
reaction. Doubtless the situation in the twentieth century
was a different situation, and there was no danger of a
recrudescence of Gallicanism in the precise form of the
eighteenth century. But the twentieth century had given
its evidence that, while there was perhaps a need for de-

centralization, there was also a danger in it. Formidable logic might demonstrate that the world with its improvement of communications was now one, that the days of old-fashioned nationalism had gone, and that a World Authority was required; but in fact nationalism was stronger than it had ever been, and it was absurd to overlook the possibility that if large powers were given to national episcopacies, nationalism might reassert itself even in the religious field—if not in the form of old-fashioned Gallicanism perhaps in a form even more evil and dangerous.

The two great wars of the twentieth century had both shown how strong was the force of nationalism over the modern mind and how rare it was to find an ecclesiastical leader who at a time of international crisis was capable of rising above a purely national point of view. In the 1914 War, for instance, all the national bishops in every country of the world, with hardly an exception, rallied with monotonous obedience to their country's cause; those on the Allied side supported the Allies, those on the German side supported the Germans, and those in neutral countries pleaded for neutrality. The only voice that was raised in clear criticism of the tragedy of events—that pointed out without equivocation the need for bringing Europe's folly to a quick end if Europe's hegemony was not to be destroyed—was that of Benedict XV.

The experience of the war by no means showed that it was safe to entrust the fortunes of the Catholic Church entirely to national hierarchies. In present times, however desirable it may be to allow wide measures of administrative decentralization to the hierarchies of so-called free countries, certainly the faithful in totalitarian countries, where bishops cannot speak freely or perhaps cannot speak at all, are grateful that there is a voice at Rome that the totalitarian rulers cannot reach and cannot still. The dangers of an excessive collegiality and too reckless a de-

centralization were dramatically emphasized at this session by a speech from Archbishop Slipyi. Archbishop
Slipyi was the Ukrainian bishop who at the time of the
first session had been released from a long and cruel period of imprisonment in Siberia, where many of his colleagues had died. He made a speech pleading passionately
for the retention of a strong central voice in Rome to
urge the cause of those who suffered under totalitarian
regimes. Oriental Catholics protested against the tend-
ency of the Westerners to speak as if the Catholic Church
consisted only of Catholics of the Latin rite. The issue of
Vatican II, wrote Father Tavard, member of the Secretariat for Christian Unity, in *La Croix* is Will the Church be
Catholic or simply Latin? But they did not ask for a dimi-
nution of the authority of the pope. They merely asked
that the pope use his authority to protect them in their
undoubted rights.

It was, therefore, not unreasonable that the Council
should in these matters move somewhat slowly nor that
the pope should have shown no anxiety to push things to a
too rapid conclusion before every point of view had been
fully discussed. The main work of this second session was
still the work that was being done in commissions. The
full Assembly was asked only to express guiding judge-
ments on particular points from time to time, and it was
wise not to hurry the commissions. So, in general, the time
had not yet come for the consideration of detailed amendments to the schemata; yet one important point of principle came before it. Should the teaching about Mary be
incorporated in a separate schema, or should it be included in the schema on the Church? There was, of
course, no difference of opinion among the Fathers about
the honour due to the Mother of God nor any sort of demand that the pronouncements about the Immaculate
Conception and the Assumption should in any way be
abrogated. It might therefore seem that the exact docu-

ment in which the Fathers' tribute to Mary was expressed
was of secondary importance. This was not wholly so.
While no Catholic challenges the Church's teaching
about Mary, there were those, disciples of what is known
as the Marian Movement, who called for further definitions that would recognize Mary as the sole channel of
graces and the like. Such movements were to be found particularly in Italy and other South European countries.
Theologians elsewhere thought that there was a danger
in these extravagances. If Mary was the Mother of God,
no man of sense would wish to declare any marvel about
her to be impossible or indeed even improbable; but there
is nothing that we can reasonably say about the details
of the next life or of the manner in which grace acts except that we do not know how such things work, and it
would be dangerous to impose as an obligatory dogma
further beliefs about our Lady in heaven that Catholics
had done without for two thousand years; for it cannot
seriously be argued that there is any scriptural warrant
for such things, and their meaning is not wholly comprehensible to man in his present state. It is one thing to accept mysteries that God has revealed and has bidden us
to accept. It is quite another to invent mysteries for ourselves.

As in the previous session the integralists had wished
to state that Tradition was the one source of Doctrine
and progressives, unwilling to affront Protestants of
good will unnecessarily, had asked that the authority of
Scripture be also recognized, so now the progressives argued that what is commonly called mariolatry—the as-
cription to Mary of new and extravagant titles—is one
of the main obstacles to the reunion of the Catholic
Church with other Christian denominations. Insofar as the
obstacle is caused by a refusal of the other denominations
to accept the position of honour the Catholic Church ac-
cords to our Lady, there is nothing to do but to regret-

fully accept it as an irremovable obstacle. We cannot abate from our essential position. But, on the other hand, the Protestant Churches accept the creeds that assert the Virgin Birth. The Protestants are often repelled not by essential Catholic doctrine but by the extravagance of practice and phraseology indulged in by some Catholics; and there can be no question that it is possible to find examples at which they are right to be repelled. In his inaugural address to the second session Pope Paul took the opportunity to remind the world that according to Catholic teaching it was Christ who was the head of the Church and upon whom it was founded. Those bishops who were most keenly alive to the ecumenical duty of the Council and who thought that every opportunity should be taken to hasten the day when all Christians should be one thought that it would be a mistake to put the Church's teaching on Mary into a separate schema because that would imply that it was different from its teaching on other topics and on the nature of the Church in general. The extreme Marians, of course, thought the opposite. On a vote the ecumenists carried the day but only by a narrow majority—by 1,114 votes to 1,074. It was by far the closest of all the Council's votes. As a general rule, by the time of the votes so much trouble had been taken to meet the difficulties of objectors that the actual divisions showed something approaching unanimity. But in this case it was not so.

The pope accepted the vote of the majority, and the Marian definitions were included in the general schema on the Church. But the pope later threw a certain sop to the minority by giving Mary the title of "Mother of the Church" in the schema on ecumenism—an honorific title that clearly had no specific meaning, a title that could therefore give little offence, even though at the same time it is not easy to think that it gave any very special pleasure or served any great purpose.

It was the determination of Pope Paul as much as it had been the determination of his predecessor that this Council, in contrast to some previous Councils, should be a free Council. This meant that it must be a slow-moving Council. It meant that bishops must be prepared to come to it not with preconceived notions but with minds as nearly open as possible, prepared to listen and to learn from others with experience different from their own, anxious as far as possible not to marshal a majority to vote down the minority but to discover a unanimous general mind of the Church, which would not be a mere highest common factor of convenience but the will of the Holy Ghost. This policy presented Pope Paul with a problem to some extent the opposite of that of Pope John. Pope John called for an *aggiornamento* of the Church in face of a curial opposition that was commonly thought to be complacently content with things as they were and to be opposed to reform. The first task was to ensure that the progressives got a fair hearing. By Pope Paul's time the problem was largely the opposite problem. The votes of the Assembly clearly showed that it was the progressives who were in the overwhelming majority, and the pope's main concern was to persuade them to make their demands in a tactful way, to understand the values of tradition, and above all not to rob the pope of the final voice that the Church had so often needed in the past and which it was likely to need again in the future.

The two definite achievements of this session were the decree on the liturgy and the decree on the mass communications media. Of the principle on which liturgical reform was based I have already spoken. The principle had been substantially accepted at the first session. The decree based upon it was passed at the second session almost unanimously. Only four votes were cast against it, and on January 25th, 1964, by a *motu proprio* the pope published the general rules for its application. The constitu-

tion lays down "the general principle for the restoration
and promotion of the sacred liturgy." "Christ's purpose,"
says its first chapter, "was that the apostles might accom-
plish the work of salvation which they proclaimed by
means of sacrifice and sacraments, around which the
entire liturgical life revolves." Therefore it is the duty of
the priests to see that the faithful "take part fully aware
of what they are doing, actively engaged in the rites and
enriched by its effects." Private prayer is, of course, still
encouraged, but the member of a congregation should not
indulge in private prayer in indifference to a public
service he is attending. Echoing and reinforcing the words
of Pius XII's *Mediator*, the decree calls for the "full, conscious and active participation" of all the faithful. Fuller
liturgical training for seminarists is called for. It is
stressed that still further reforms besides those here enu-
merated will certainly be needed, and the details of them
are remitted to a liturgical commission; but the general
principles of reform should be three. First, the primacy
of Scripture should be emphasized. The reading of Scripture should play a larger part in the Church's worship,
and by reading it in the vernacular, the congregation
should better understand it. The Council advises the use
of special Bible services "especially on the vigils of the
more solemn feasts, on some weekdays of Advent and
Lent and on Sundays and feast days." Since the purpose
of rites is to inform the spirit of the people, they should
be "short, clear and unencumbered by useless repetition
. . . within the people's power of comprehension and
normally should not require much explanation." Com-
plexities should be excised. Third, the communal nature of worship must be reasserted. "Liturgical services,"
said the decree, "are not private functions but are celebra-
tions of the Church," which is "the sacrament of unity,"
namely "the holy people united and ordered under their
bishops." Therefore, liturgical services pertain to the

whole body of the Church. "When there is the possibility of a general celebration involving the presence and active participation of the people, this way of celebrating them is to be preferred." Participation by the congregation is in every way to be encouraged. A dialogue Mass is recommended. The congregation should be encouraged "to take part by means of acclamations, responses, psalmody, antiphons and hymns, as well as by actions, gestures, and bodily attitudes." Each person present is to do "all of, but only, those parts which pertain to his office by the nature of the rite and the principles of the liturgy."

Apart from the introduction of the actual vernacular language, the national hierarchies are encouraged to introduce national adaptations into their particular liturgies. Nothing very much has come of this up to the present, but what the Fathers seem to have intended was that in mission countries there should be a recognition of local customs where habitual gestures and the like might have a different significance from those with which they are accustomed. The full use of the vernacular languages was of course recommended. "One should address God," said Abbot Butler of Downside, "in the language in which one makes love." Wherever possible the priest should say Mass not with his back to the congregation as if he was excluding them from a mystery but facing them. The custom of concelebration was licensed and a reform of the breviary ordered. "The accounts of martyrdoms or lives of the saints are to accord with the facts of history."

The task of working out the details was once more remitted to the various national hierarchies. As is known, schemes have been produced and put in operation in all countries but are still in the experimental stage. At present there is in almost all countries a somewhat strange medley of Latin and vernacular, and it is of course one thing to licence the vernacular and another to produce a worthy and widely acceptable vernacular version. But in general it may be said that these reforms are not, as is sometimes said, a revolution. They are rather a return behind those customs that were imposed by the Council of Trent to meet problems that are no longer with us and behind certain medieval and late medieval customs to something much more like the primitive forms of worship. It is a renewal, not a revolution.

The second decree of the second session—that on mass communications media—was of a very different order of importance from the decree on the liturgy. Just as at the first session, this schema had been the first whose draft received the approval of the Council, not because it was the most important and the most impressive but perhaps because it was one of the least important and therefore the least controversial and the Fathers were anxious to produce some evidence of achievement; so it was perhaps with something of the same attitude that the draft was submitted to the General Assembly in this session. But there was no very great enthusiasm for it among the Fathers. When it was first submitted on November 25th, 1963, it received only 1,598 votes against 503. In view of the opposition it was revised and somewhat shortened; the revised form did somewhat better, being passed by 1,960 to 164 on December 4th. But even so it was not a very impressive document and was passed more because the Fathers were anxious to be rid of it than because they were greatly enamoured of it. By general agreement it was the least distinguished of the Council's documents. It was, therefore, unfortunate that it should have been the first.

In a somewhat vague and platitudinous way it calls for active Catholic work in the press, films, radio, and television—which doubtless no one disputes. As for whether it is better for Catholics to have their own organs of opinion or to work in collaboration with others, it can say nothing more exciting than that all depends on circumstances. What more indeed could one say if one was to issue a generalization addressed impartially to all the world? But if no more can be said, is so much worth saying? It shows a certain favour for specifically Catholic papers and programmes where they are possible but recognizes that they are often not possible. In fact, the need for a specifically Catholic press depends very much on how far the secular press is willing to give full and fair accounts of Catholic events. If they are fully reported in the secular press, they obviously reach many people who would never have heard of them if they had been reported in Catholic papers only. It is certainly true that very largely owing to Pope John and to the good will and interest the Council has aroused, Catholic doings are today reported in all countries much more fully than they were a few years ago. But it would be difficult to give evidence of any new development that has been the consequence of this schema.

The truth undoubtedly was that the majority of bishops were not familiar with the techniques of mass media, and there was a pretty general feeling that they had spoken on this matter only because they felt that it was expected of them and not because they had anything particular to say. The hard-boiled journalists thought that on this matter it was of more importance to look to the actual treatment of the press at the Council than to the theoretical resolutions of the Fathers. They found that the press facilities afforded to them were less satisfactory than those they would have received at an international secular conference, but those of them who were acquainted with history understood how great a breach it was with Vatican tradition to grant any facilities to the press at all and contrasted what was, not with what might have been, but with what would have been in any previous age. Others were generous enough to recognize that the facilities, though to the end far from ideal, at least improved considerably as the Council went on.

The second session showed most evidently that the

Council had not yet solved its problems of procedure. The new pope was at first as reluctant as Pope John had been to interfere in any way with the fullest freedom of debate. It was clear that if group organizations were allowed to form themselves and one man allowed to speak not merely in his own person but in the names of others, there was a certain danger that eccentric opinions would be crowded out; and eccentric opinions, though often of little value, do on some occasions prove to be wiser than the opinions of the Establishment. In any event, it would certainly violate the principle of a free Council to prevent the expression of any view. Nevertheless, it became clear as time went on that some group organization of opinion was essential if anything was going to be done and intolerable repetition to be avoided. To what extent things happened as they did by accident and to what extent by plan is even yet not quite certain, but the way things worked out was clearly the best way. For a time debate was allowed to run free. During that time anyone could speak. Final decisions were not reached, but the Fathers had the opportunity both to learn from the full gamut of opinions that were held by their colleagues and also to decide for themselves who among those colleagues had the gift of leadership. When the leaders had shown themselves, then it was more possible to look for group organizations, to appoint spokesmen, and to decide that the time for concrete progress had come. More exact definitions of the relative functions of the various officials—the moderators, the Presidency Commission, the Coordinating Commissions, and the General Council—were made. In his closing address the pope called for an abbreviation and concentrating of the remaining schemata. At that time he obviously hoped that the third session would be more fruitful than the first or second.

It had, as has been said, at first not been quite certain whether an ecumenical Council was going to mean a council of the Catholic bishops of all the world or a council of the different denominations. It turned out that the first was the correct meaning; but at the same time Pope John and Pope Paul were always, of course, mindful that a main purpose of the Council was to bring nearer the day of Christian unity and that the Council would very largely have failed if nothing was achieved in that direction. Therefore, observers from all the other denominations were invited. Most of them accepted, and all were treated with conspicuous courtesy. Very properly, the other denominations had for the most part chosen as their observers men of good will but men whose ecclesiastical position was not notably close to that of the Catholic Church. Little purpose would have been served if men had been chosen who were already suspect in their own communions and who would have been criticized within them as having sold out had they made what were interpreted as excessive concessions to the Roman position. The very fact that the men chosen were notably not of that sort made the tributes they were able to pay to the treatment they received all the more valuable. The spirit of the Council was in this respect the spirit of Pope John—a spirit of the dialogue of courtesy.

It was wholly to the good that the spirit of ill will should have been entirely absent from the Council. As a result of the dialogue of courtesy the observers were, one may hope, able to carry away a good opinion of Catholic courtesy; but quite apart from that the educative effect on the bishops was immeasurable. As has been said, the educative consequences of the Council may well in general prove to be its most important effects. It did bishops great good to learn what other bishops were like. But it did them perhaps even more good to learn what non-Catholics were like. Up till then so many of them had lived almost entirely in the company of their coreligionists. They knew nothing of what non-Catholics were like save what they had read of them in print. Pope John, whose experience of mankind was so much wider than that of most ecclesiastics, had already reminded us in *Pacem in Terris* that those who had "a false philosophy" might nevertheless be often responsible for good actions and that it was desirable to cooperate with others with whom one could not wholly agree. Nevertheless, the problem of interdenominational relations was not, and could not be, an easy one. For it was, of course, the inevitable belief of the members of other denominations that they belonged to the Catholic Church.

It was equally inevitable that the Catholics, from their very title deeds, could not fully grant that claim. They could recognize the validity of the non-Catholics' baptism. They could admit fully the sincerity of their Christian faith. They could take care to use words as inoffensive as possible to describe them, be careful to speak of "separated brethren" and the like, where earlier generations would not have hesitated to say "heretics." Pope Paul did not hesitate to admit that Catholics must bear their large share of responsibility for the disunion that had fallen upon Christendom. Yet in the last resort in his inaugural address he could not but say of those "other Christians, those who believe in Christ but whom we have not the happiness of numbering among ourselves in the perfect unity of Christ which only the Catholic Church can offer them" that "the Church of Christ is one alone and therefore must be unique" and that "this mystic and visible union cannot be attained save in identity of faith and by participation in the same sacraments and in the organic harmony of a single ecclesiastical direction." Although it is not easy to see how a pope could have spoken otherwise than this, yet it is certain that these frank words did create a certain disappointment among some of those of other denominations, and there were among them those who felt that Pope Paul, in contrast to Pope John, had not really any belief in a unity save one in submission to himself. But, any belief that he was half-hearted in his pursuit of Christian reunion was dramatically disproved when at the conclusion of the second session he announced that he would in the next days pay a visit to Jerusalem and meet there the Ecumenical Patriarch. By this gesture the faith of Christians was renewed.

CHAPTER IV

THE THIRD SESSION

The third session was to be the session for practical decisions. Many people hoped that it might be possible to bring the Council to a conclusion. There is some reason to think that the pope had such a hope. In the event, it proved that the Council was able to pass during the session three drafts —on the Constitution of the Church, on Oriental Rites and on Ecumenism—but at its conclusion these still remained either for debate or at least for voting one draft of a constitution, six draft decrees, the famous Schema XIII on the Church and the Modern World, three draft declarations, and one votum of petition. All these were discussed during the third session, although final conclusions on them were not reached. The Schema on Bishops, which at first appeared as "On the Bishops and the Government of Dioceses" and was then rechristened "On the Pastoral Duties of the Bishops in the Church," was put to the vote, but of its three chapters only one received the necessary two-thirds majority. It had, therefore, to go back to its commission for redrafting. The schemata on the Priesthood, on the Missions, and on The Renewal of Religious Life were also rejected and sent back for redrafting. The propositions on the Formation of Priests and on Christian Education were both passed but with a number of reservations that required the insertion of amendments. The votum on Marriage was passed by a majority and sent to the pope.

Other schemata—on Revelation, on the Apostolate of the Laity—had not gotten as far as the final form for submission to the Assembly before the session ended. The declaration on the Relationship of the Church to Non-Christian Churches was accepted at its first reading by an overwhelming majority, and the Assembly left final drafting of the amendments to the fourth session. But the unexpected obstacles that caused the session to end in a state almost of tumult were the quite unforeseen difficulty encountered in passing the declaration on Religious Liberty and that on the Jews. The American bishops, as has been said, attached especial importance to the declaration on Religious Liberty. It was, said Father Courtney Murray, "the American theological question of the Council." The Americans thought it essential in order to enable them and other Catholics to refute the charge that the Catholic Church pleaded for liberty for itself when it was in the minority but denied it to others when it was in the majority. In consequence, the most disastrous outcome of all would be that there should be a suggestion of a declaration of religious liberty, that the bishops should be deceived into telling non-Catholics that it would pass, and that then some procedural manoeuvre should prevent it from being put to the vote. Yet this was what appeared to be happening when the revised text, which had been prepared by the Secretariat of Unity as early as October 24th, was not distributed to the Fathers until November 17th and it was then announced that since there was not time for a full consideration of the revised text, a vote on it could not be taken this session. The pope was compelled to promise that a vote on it would be the first business of the next session. There were many both within and without the Assembly who asserted that it was the intention of certain bishops in the curia and from Southern Europe to see that by one procedural device or another it would never be voted on at all. Had there been any attempt to postpone the vote still further when the Assembly met for its fourth session, the result might have been really serious.

There was a not dissimilar danger of a real outburst of revolt about the handling of the declaration on the Jews. It was obvious both on the general principles of Christianity and on the ecumenical principles by which the Council was professing to regulate its conduct that the Council must make it clear that the Catholic had a duty to love all men and therefore a duty among others to love all Jews. It might, it is true, have been argued that this was so obvious that it was not worth making a special statement about. However, the record of Christian treatment of Jews throughout the ages was such that many thought that it was desirable that the Council should make some special statement of repudiation of anti-Semitism. Accusations against the Jews had been so sadly common throughout the generations of Christian history that such a statement was, it seemed to many, most certainly called for; and when one remembered the terrible story of the treatment of Jews only a few years before it could not be pretended that anti-Semitism was so completely a thing of the distant past that there was no call for its special repudiation today. It is true, of course, that the Nazi leaders were not in any way Catholics and therefore the principles of Catholicism could not in any way be held responsible for their atrocities. But it was unfortunately also true that a fearful number of the Nazi leaders, with Hitler at their head, were men who had been brought up as Catholics. Nor was it possible to forget that not so many years before the Nazis, in France at the time of the Dreyfus case, an appallingly large part in the anti-Semitic campaign there had been the work of *enragés* Catholics. Therefore it was thought necessary that the Council should issue a forthright repudiation in the name of Catholicism of all prejudice against Jews.

If such a statement was to be issued, it was obviously of

the first importance that it should be as strong as possible and that it should have gone through quickly, without question and without opposition. Unfortunately, this is by no means what happened. The notion that because of the actions of a few Jews at the time of the crucifixion the Jews in general were a cursed "deicide" race and that by the crucifixion they had forfeited their right to be the Chosen People was clearly a fantastic notion. Even at the time of the crucifixion the number of Jews who were in any way associated with the killing of Christ was very small. The High Priests of that day, so far from being representatives of the Jewish people at large, were rather an unpopular "Quisling" group of Sadducees who were in power because they had preferred the Roman cause to that of their own people. The Jewish nation even of their own day could no more be held responsible for the chief priests' actions than the Norwegian nation could be held responsible for the actions of a few collaborators at the time of the German occupation; and to hold the Jews of today—decent law-abiding citizens walking the streets of Manchester or of New York—as in some way responsible for what was done two thousand years ago was hardly sane. A few fanatics thought it right to condemn them on the ground that the crowds before Pilate shouted, "His blood be upon us and on our children!" They overlooked the fact that it was indeed a Jewish habit to hold children responsible for the deeds of their parents but that Christ explicitly repudiated such beliefs when he said, "Father, forgive them for they know not what they do." Whether on general Christian principles or on biblical authority, it would be impossible to imagine any doctrine that was more explicitly condemned than the doctrine of anti-Semitism.

To the overwhelming majority of the Fathers this was clear enough. But strangely and most unfortunately there was a small minority, among whom Bishop Carli of Segni was especially prominent, who insisted on championing the worst of the old medieval traditions and asserting the guilt of the Jewish race. These eccentrics would not in themselves have been sufficient to have held up the decision of the Council. Unfortunately, they found allies in the bishops from the Arab countries. There is little reason to think that these Arab bishops were much interested in the perverted theological argument. Their fear was the more natural, if unfortunate, fear that a consequence of a decision of the Council repudiating anti-Semitism would be interpreted, however strongly it was asserted that the issues were entirely unconnected with one another, as a gesture of support for the political state of Israel. As a consequence, feared these Arab Christians, Christians in the Arab countries would be looked on by the Moslem rulers of these countries as friends of their countries' enemies and as a consequence would suffer.

First, these Arabs were able to bring sufficient pressure to bear to ensure that if the Council made a statement of friendship to Jews, such a statement should be accompanied by, and included in, the same document as a statement of friendship for other non-Christian religions and particularly for the Mohammedan religion. There was no objection to this in itself, even though it would clearly have been a great deal more satisfactory if the Fathers could have decided how they were going to handle the problem in private before it came to public debate. It did nothing but harm that the first proposal should have been to treat the problem in one way and that after some acrimonious public debate the Council should have decided to treat it in a different way. Not only was it agreed that the repudiation of anti-Semitism should be included in a general document containing a repudiation of hostility to other non-Christian religions as well, but certain changes in wording were also accepted.

These changes were of no great moment in themselves, and if their wording had been the wording first proposed, they would have aroused no great excitement. But all the changes were in the direction of slightly watering down the phraseology of the Council's repudiation. The word "deicide," for instance, was cut out of the text. All these changes were unfortunate, and what was even more unfortunate was that as a result of the negotiations the vote was not taken at the third session as it had been confidently affirmed that it would be taken, and the Council dissolved amid bitter rumours that it would never be taken. Here again the fourth session was fortunately able to redeem the reputation of the Council at least partially, and the vote, in spite of the dark rumours, was in fact taken before the Council finally dissolved; but for this reason as much as for the failure to make the assertion of religious liberty, the third session of the Council broke up in a mood of some bitterness.

Indeed, one must face the fact that there were during this third session ominous signs of a certain tension between the pope and an important section of the Fathers. They came to suggest that the pope was not playing fair with their texts. The pope added what was called a *nota explicativa praevia* to their decree on Collegiality, which they alleged greatly weakened its force. The pope inserted the title of *Mater Ecclesiae* (Mother of the Church) into the chapter on Mary in the schema on *Ecumenism,* though this title had been explicitly avoided in the Fathers' final drafting on the ground that a large number of the Fathers had objected to it. In his final allocution the pope gave a picture of a relationship between the pope and the bishops that seemed to many of the bishops exceptionally papalistic. Whether the pope handled the matter as adroitly as he could have handled it is a matter for debate. But he was, as has been indicated, in a position of some difficulty.

Demands for an administrative decentralization from the control of overcentralized Rome were reasonable, and the bishops had the right to assert that their own authority was of divine ordination and not derived through Rome. Still, some of the bishops were without doubt men of short memories and of little knowledge of history. It was desirable to assure them that under any normal circumstances they would have a wide measure of freedom. Yet the memory of Benedict XV—without going into more ancient memories of Gallicanism—could not be wholly erased. There were occasions when local bishops had proved wiser than the popes, but there were other occasions when the local bishops had proved not so very wise— had failed to rise above national prejudice—when it was well that there should be a voice at Rome that could speak fearlessly *urbi et orbi*. Such occasions might occur again. But the objection was not so much to the content of the *nota explicativa praevia* in itself as to the way in which it was published. It was published in the *Osservatore Romano* as an adjunct to the Schema on the Church and, according to a communication made by the Secretary General, was to form part of the Acts of the Council. It was objected that, pertinent as it might be, this *nota* had never been submitted or voted on by the Council and was in no proper way a part of the Acts of the Council. Much of the same objection was raised to the insertion of the title of the Mother of the Church, *Mater Ecclesiae,* in the chapter on Mary. The title was clearly an honorific title with no specific meaning. It could make no substantial difference whether it was there or not, but, at the time of the redrafting of the chapter, many of the Fathers had objected to it for just that reason. They thought that the Church made itself ridiculous by honorific language that had no meaning. John XXIII had greatly discouraged the use of phrases of meaningless and hyperbolical compliment in addressing the pope, and almost all the Fathers had applauded when Pope Paul's firm insistence on Christ's leadership of the Church at his inaugural address had seemed to convey a rebuke to those extreme Mariologists who encouraged exaggerated language about the Mother of God. The insertion of this title was clearly a sop to the Mariologists. It made a verbal gesture to them without conceding any real point and was therefore in tune with the pope's general policy of preventing the Council from becoming in any way a trampling ground of victors over vanquished. But there were some who wondered whether it was altogether dignified that honorific titles to the Mother of God should be used for such a purpose.

In public session on November 21st three decrees were passed: on the Constitution of the Church, on the Catholic Oriental Churches, and on Ecumenism. Of these that of the Catholic Orientals was both the least important and perhaps the least satisfactory. It is obviously one of the problems of ecumenism that the more generous the language that is used about those outside the Catholic Church, the greater the danger of giving offence to those who in the same circumstances have remained loyal Catholics and kept the non-Catholics at arm's length in the belief that by doing so they were displaying their loyalty to the pope. Thus in Great Britain the English Catholics in the years after the First World War cold-shouldered Cardinal Mercier's plans for conversations at Malines with Anglican representatives, arguing that Anglican orders had been condemned by Leo XIII and that the Anglican claims were clearly incompatible with any Catholic position and that discussion must therefore necessarily be fruitless. Modern developments such as the pope speaking directly to the Archbishop of Canterbury and Anglican observers attending the Council by invitation have caused certain difficulties to the English Catholic bishops, making them appear more intransigent towards Anglicans than the pope.

It was a somewhat similar position, though the details were different, concerning papal relations with the Eastern Church. The Orthodox were, of course, in schism,

rejecting the authority of the pope even though their orders were recognized by Rome as valid. The Catholic
Orientals, on the other hand, while retaining their own
rites, had yet remained in communion with Rome. Naturally enough there was a certain danger that an excessive
rapprochement with the Orthodox might cause a certain
resentment among the Oriental Catholics who would fear
that people would be tempted to say, "If the pope thinks so
highly of the Orthodox Church, what point can there be in
leaving it in order to join the Catholic rite?"

What was important was to reassure the Oriental Catholics that there was no intention of attacking their privileges or attempting to Latinize them. Earlier drafts had
used language that seemed to identify the Church with
Catholics of the Latin rite. As has already been quoted,
Father Tavard had asked the question, "Will the Church
be Catholic or simply Latin?" The purpose of the schema
on the Oriental Catholics was to preserve a balance, to
show that the Church for all its ecumenical sympathies was
not prepared to accept anyone irrespective of his beliefs
and at the same time did not draw its boundaries too nar-
rowly and insist on the abrogation by loyal Catholics of
their traditional privileges. The Orientals were reassured
in their privileges. The Patriarchs were promised that
their full rights, as before the Schism, would be restored.
As for *communicatio in sacris* with Orthodox, the canoni-
cal form of marriage, it was decided, was required only
for the lawfulness—not for the validity—of the marriage.
Any marriage was valid if a sacred minister was present.
Thus the marriage of an Oriental Catholic before an Orthodox priest would be valid but not lawful. If it is physi-
cally impossible to get to a priest of one's own sort, then
it is permitted either for Oriental Catholics to receive communion from an Orthodox or for an Oriental Catholic
priest to give communion to an Orthodox. All "these
laws," it was voted, "hold good only till the Catholic

Church and the separated Oriental Churches unite in the fullness of communion." Cardinal Lercaro had suggested that it would be wiser for the Council to have left it to the local patriarchs to lay down their rules for *communicatio in sacris* and not to have attempted to regulate such matters from Rome. But this suggestion was not followed.

Of very much more general importance were the two decrees—in some ways interconnected—on the Church and on Ecumenism. First, what exactly is the Church? According to Catholic belief Christ, the Son of God, founded a Church to which all men were bidden to join themselves. On the other hand, he also manifestly died not for Catholics alone but for all men. What does the Church teach about those who do not accept its message? And what in particular does it teach about those who accept the Divinity of Christ but cannot find his teaching exclusively in the Roman Catholic Church?

It almost stands to reason that the decree on the Constitution of the Church was the central achievement of the Council, for only when it had been settled what the Church was did it make any sense to discuss what should be its relation to those outside it. The decree falls into two parts. The first part consists of four chapters—on the Mystery of the Church, on the People of God, on the hierarchical structure of the Church, and on the laity. The four other chapters are accessory. They are on the general vocation to holiness in the Church, on the religious orders, on eschatological teaching and the relation of the Church on earth to the Church in heaven, and on Mary. One of these accessory chapters, chapter V, on the call to holiness was proposed from the first. While the Church was calling, and rightly calling, on the faithful to play their part along with their non-Catholic fellow citizens as good citizens, it was necessary to preserve the balance, to remind them that while the Church of God who came down into this world was, in contrast to some other religious bodies, necessarily concerned with the affairs of this world, it was not exclusively concerned with them. It was the Catholic's duty to be a good citizen, but it was not his first duty to be a good citizen. It was his first duty to love God, and it was from the performance of that duty that all other virtues would follow. In the order of reason, it was by no means self-evident that a man should love all his fellow men. Only the very greatest of saints have even begun to do so. Most of us can at the most only claim to have loved—to have made our will one with—a very few people, and it is only because we recognize others as the fellow creatures of God that we even think that we have a duty to love them. We love our neighbour in the order of reason because we love God. But in the order of experience it is the other way round. If we had not gotten some glimpse of it from love of a fellow man, how should we ever have come to guess that such a thing as love existed? "He who loveth not his neighbour whom he hath seen, how shall he love God whom he hath not seen?"

The three accessory chapters had not been intended at the time of the first drafting. They arose without premeditation as a conequence of the debates and to meet particular objections. When it was proclaimed that all men and women had both an invitation to and a possibility of holiness, common language that spoke of those who lived in religion as living in "a state of perfection" with an implication that those who lived a secular life were living in a state of imperfection could no longer be accepted. On the other hand, the religious had clearly a right to ask for an answer from the Council to those who from such assertions might ask about what purpose there is in people shutting themselves up in monasteries or convents if they can live lives that are just as Christian outside them? It was on the demand of bishops from religious Orders and of Superior Generals in the Council that a chapter was inserted to show that although people in every walk of life could and should remember the eschatological nature of the Church's promises, yet the pressure of worldliness was to the ordinary man and woman so great that it was a good thing and pleasing to the will of God that some people should visibly and indeed almost ostentatiously devote themselves to the unworldly life.

The chapter on the eschatological nature of the Christian promises was also, it seems, an afterthought. It was put in to make clear the Fathers' rejection of what Bishop de Smedt had called "triumphalism," the belief that it was a part of Catholic loyalty to pretend that the Church was winning all its battles over the world and, still more, that it was a sort of political party and that a Catholic was necessarily doing his duty as a Catholic if he automatically took the so-called Catholic side in every worldly controversy that turned up and in which a Catholic happened to be involved. The Christian religion was concerned about deeper things than that; and human beings were not simply divided into black and white according to whether they were Catholic or non-Catholic. The chapter on Mary, as has already been said, was inserted as an alternative to having a separate decree on Mary. It is perhaps not altogether satisfactory, but at least while naturally insisting on the Church's devotion to Mary, it does contain an admission that there have been wrong forms of devotion to her and demands that these be remedied.

The main chapters of the decree are more important. One can look at them as an exercise in careful balance. In the early chapters the traditional teaching that the Church is a Church of authority is repeated. The fourth chapter—that on the laity—makes it clear, however, that this does not mean that the laity in any way belong to the clergy. Authority is real, but it is not absolute. It had never been the intention of the First Vatican Council to suggest that it was the pope alone who had any authority in the Church. If that impression was conveyed to some people and if perhaps as a result of it the centralized authority of the papacy has increased in the ninety odd years since the First Vatican Council, that is simply the result of an historical accident—of the accident that the Council considered first the position of the pope and then before it had time to pass on to further points on its agenda, to the consideration of the position of bishops, priests, and of the laity, it was dissolved by the Franco-Prussian War. Yet whether one looks at it from the dogmatic or from the pragmatic point of view, it is obvious that it is not the pope alone who enjoys authority from God. The Gospels tell us that Peter was divinely appointed as the head of the apostles, but there is no suggestion that the other eleven in any way derived their authority from him. They derived their authority directly from Christ. So today a bishop is a bishop in his own right. He exercises his office by divine authority. The bishops form a college of their own. A priest derives his authority from an ordination that comes formally from the hands of the bishop but which carries with it the grace of the Holy Spirit. The laity are the people of God. All in their various degrees are under the pope, but the pope is not by himself the Church. The Church is the pope, the bishops, the priests, and the laity. It comprises them all.

Similarly on the pragmatic plane. An absolutist regime, whether it be of Church or State, means in fact that power is not so much in the hands of the absolute ruler as in the hands of the bureaucrats. Only the most remarkable and energetic of monarchs can in reality keep all power in his own hands—and then usually with disastrous results. Autocracy means that a vast volume of appeals from every corner of the Empire find their way to the capital and are there dealt with by the bureaucrats. It was the same with Rome. Rulings on trivial cases could not be taken by local episcopal courts but had to be referred to Rome, where decisions were given only after intolerable delay. This

would in any event have been a grave evil, calling for redress. But so long as the Catholic body was a small body
predominantly resident in Western Europe, then those
who forwarded their petitions to the Italian authorities in
Rome were at least submitting themselves to the judgement of men who were predominantly of the same culture
as themselves. The grievance was much more serious
when the Church had become in fact, and not merely in
name, a worldwide institution and when the petitions came
from persons of a wholly different culture from that of the
judges. A Roman official might pass judgement on the
matrimonial problems of a Frenchman or a Spaniard.
What competence could he have to pass judgement on the
matrimonial problems of an Indian or a Japanese? How
could he know whether ceremonies that had taken place
in such countries and according to native custom should
properly be considered marriages?

It is true that while the chapter clearly showed that the
old Victorian notion of Mgr Talbot that the function of the
laity was solely 'to hunt, to shoot, and to entertain' was
completely abandoned, it did not make exactly clear what
the laity was to do in the new dispensation. The laity of the
modern Catholic world was in fact doing many things that
in previous generations had been left almost entirely in
clerical hands. They played a much larger part than here-
tofore in managing the financial affairs of a diocese. They
were playing an increasing part in the teaching in schools
and colleges. How far this was due to a deliberate choice
and how far to the fact that the shortage of priests made it
necessary to hand over to laymen all functions for which
the priesthood was not absolutely essential was a matter of
opinion. Pastoral councils consisting of religious and laymen, were, the chapter told us, to be set up in every
diocese, but to what extent the layman is to have any independence of ecclesiastical control, to what extent his
activities are to be confined within the fairly limited and

defined activities of Catholic Action, and to what extent
he was to be left free to interpret for himself in what direction his Catholic activities might lie was not very clear.

The original draft kept very much to the beaten path
and clearly did not wish to encourage anything that was
in the way of independent action, but it was vigorously
attacked in the debates, most notably by Archbishop
Veuillot, the Coadjutor of Paris, who said, "The Holy
Ghost has set the bishops to rule the Church of God, and
the same Holy Ghost kindles the apostolic fervour and
initiatives of the laity." On a more mundane level, in
countries where Catholics are in a minority there is of
course a place for purely Catholic organizations, but it is
clear that in an unsympathetic and uncomprehending en-
vironment the Catholic who never acts except by express
and admitted command of the hierarchy will not in fact be
able to exercise any influence in his society. Even in Catholic countries, such as Italy, the attempt to canalize all
activities of Catholics through a formal organization of
Catholic Action have by no means been universally happy.

The most bitter debate aroused by any of the issues of
this schema was that on the re-creation of a regular diaconate. As we know, the deacons were a regular order in the
early Church, but in modern times the diaconate has become a meaningless formality of the seminarian on his
road to the priesthood. It was suggested by missionary
bishops from Africa and South America that the remedy
of the present shortage of priests in those countries was to
reconstitute the order of deacons, men who without taking
on themselves the priesthood or the obligation of celibacy
would assist the priests in their work. The only reasonable objection to such a proposal would have seemed to be
the financial one. If these deacons were to be married, they
would have to be more adequately paid than missionary
priests. But, strangely, that difficulty was little discussed
in the debates. On the other hand, there was a violent out-

burst against the suggestion from a number of Italian bishops on the ground that, as Cardinal Ruffini, put it, "married deacons would inflict a grave wound on ecclesiastical celibacy." Cardinal Spellman joined in the opposition. But the most moving speech came from Bishop Kemmerer from South America. He said, "The restoration of the diaconate is our great hope; and it is the wish of many bishops in Latin America that you, Venerable Fathers, do not deprive us of this hope when the matter comes to a vote. The door is already open and, if among you there are some who do not wish to enter, we shall not force you to enter. But we graciously beg you not to close the door on us because we do want to enter. All we ask is to do so." When the matter came to the vote on October 30th, it was passed by 1,588 votes to 525.

The introduction to the Constitution makes clear the fundamental emphasis of the document. The Church is incidentally an organization of government and authority —a *societas perfecta.* There is, of course, no attempt to deny that. The Gospel is offered to all the world, but it has never been accepted by all the world in its literal form, and there is no particular reason to think that in this dispensation it ever will be so accepted. But the Church must not therefore retire to its catacombs and hide itself from the wicked world. It has a mission to redeem the world—even a world that does not accept it. Its primary role is not authoritarian but sacramental. "In Christ," it says in the introduction, "the Church is, as it were, the sacrament, that is, the sign and instrument of intimate union with God, and of the unity of the whole human race." From this it clearly followed that any merely statistical description of the Church's success or failure—such and such an increase or decrease in Easter communions, such and such a proportion of the population that is Catholic in this country or that—while it doubtless had its value, was very insufficient as a description of the Church's strength or weakness in the world. It was doubtless valuable as an antidote to false triumphalism to be reminded how small a proportion of the world was practising Catholic and in how many countries the proportion of those practising was apparently declining. But these matters, though important, are of secondary importance. It is very essential not to think them of primary importance. The really important questions are, How far is it true that the leaven is succeeding in leavening the whole lump? How far is the spirit of Christ being spread throughout the world and far beyond the boundaries of the Catholic body? Or is there reason to fear that the practising Catholics themselves are becoming infected with the spirit of worldliness and allowing their conduct to be dictated by principles different from those of Christ? If the pope can address an international assembly such as the United Nations in a way that would have been unthinkable before the war, does this mean that the world now pays more attention to the pope than it used to pay? Or does it merely mean that the world no longer feels that it needs to fear him? If Catholics can now be elected to high political positions that would have been barred to them a few years ago, does this mean that the world is more favourable to Catholics or more indifferent to them, that those outside the Church are looking to its message or that those inside the Church are more anxious to behave as if they were in no way different from other people?

Another very important statement in the introduction concerns the relationship of the Church to non-Catholic Christians. The Church has, of course, always recognized the validity of baptism, by whoever administered, and when the introduction asserted that "the Church recognizes that it is bound by many bonds to those who have been baptized," it reminded the faithful of a truth that had perhaps been sometimes little remembered in times of bitter interdenominational controversy but which had never been denied. But the following sentence that there were many outside the Church who "recognize and receive other sacraments in their own ecclesiastical communities" was more startling. It was the problem of the relationship of Catholics to non-Catholics and of the Church to other Christian denominations that aroused the keenest controversy throughout all the debates. Did the sentence quoted merely mean that the baptism of all Christians was indeed valid but that those in schism, like the Orthodox whose priests nevertheless had valid orders, of course conferred other sacraments as well, and did it mean no more than that? Was the Council merely asserting, which again no one had doubted for a long time, that those outside the Church who did what they believed in good faith, even though erroneously, to be the will of God in fact received his grace in so doing? Or was the Assembly not only recognizing that individuals outside the Church were in good faith and deserving of salvation but also recognizing that the bodies to which they belonged were in some sense "churches" and, if so, in what sense?

Some vigorous conservatives wished to pass an amendment making the Council say unequivocally, "The Church of Christ is the Catholic Church." The majority was unwilling to agree. It preferred to preserve the wording, "The Church of Christ subsists in the Catholic Church"—a not very clear sentence that seemed to imply that all those within the Catholic Church are indeed members of the Church in Christ but that the Constitution was not willing to take on itself the responsibility of giving an excluding ruling to say who was not in the Church of Christ. Such matters were the responsibility of God alone. In contrast to previous custom, the Constitution does not speak of non-Catholics as "heretics" or "schismatics" but, following the example of Pope John, as "separated brethren." It does not, it is true, exactly define which denominational bodies are to be recognized as these "separated" churches—how far among the weird and eccentric sects

its recognition extends—but at least it firmly recognizes
that there are outside the Church churches that can properly be so called. Without such a recognition any effective
advance in the direction of ecumenism would hardly have
been possible.

It is obvious that any fuller recognition of the rights of
other religious bodies must inevitably demand a recon-
sideration of the rules of mixed marriages, and indeed, as
we know, the mixed marriage has always been and still is
the largest practical difficulty to any ecumenical developments. But the Council was not at that moment prepared
to grasp that nettle. It contented itself with passing a *votum*
expressive of the hope that before the promulgation of
the reformed Code of Canon Law the pope would issue a
Motu Proprio on the subject.

If Christ died for all men and yet founded one special
Church, then it is necessary to define the relations not only
between Catholics and non-Catholics but also between
Catholics and non-Christians. The schema on the Church
faced this challenge. "Those who through no fault of their
own," it says, "are ignorant of the gospel of Christ and the
Church but still seek God sincerely and strive under the
influence of grace to do his will as seen in the dictates of
conscience can attain to eternal salvation." There is, it
may very well be said, no great novelty in this. Most people believed that long before the Council was thought of.
It was only perhaps a little comforting to be formally reassured that it was Catholic teaching, but where the Council did break new ground was in refusing to content itself
with merely saying that there were good men outside the
bounds of Christendom who were good because of their
inherent virtue and who adhered to the religions in which
they had been brought up because they knew no better.
It goes forward to assert, to quote the phrase of Cardinal
Frings, "a redemptive process" in these non-Christian
religions. Virtuous men who profess them are virtuous not

in spite of but because of their religion. The salvific action of Christ is at work everywhere in the world—even in non-Christian religions. It does not confine itself to Christianity. It is true that the tribute to the Moslem, the Buddhist, and the Hindu religions were as a matter of fact largely introduced because it was desired to pay a tribute to the Jews and it was then thought necessary to pay tributes to other religions in order to show that the Jews were not receiving a special favour. Insofar as this was true, it was not an especially edifying reason, but it was an example that deeds are sometimes better than the motives that produce them.

If the collegiality of bishops was to be more than an empty phrase, certain practical reforms were necessary, and although they were not actually implemented at the third session, the Fathers left after having passed *vota* for the pope to implement them, and, though the details had not then, and indeed to a large extent have not yet, been announced, there was a fairly clear understanding that they would be forthcoming. Basically these demands were for a senate of bishops and for a reform of the curia. The major reform called for in the curia is that it should become less overwhelmingly Italian, but it is a reform more easily voted for than implemented. The difficulty is to get non-Italians to join it, and such few foreigners as are attracted are apt to become more Italian than the Italians themselves. The pope had appointed Cardinal Roberti to initiate inquiries into the reform of the curia, and in November, 1964, he presented a report to the College of Cardinals in the presence of the pope. The contents of it were, however, kept secret, and the details of reform were postponed until after the Council. In a similar fashion two postconciliar commissions were set up for the reform of canon law and a *Consilium Particulare* for the further reform of the liturgy. But it is still far from clear what will be the relationship between these commissions and the curial

bodies. Will they work side by side? In the event of conflict, which will be the master of the other? It depends
largely on whether the diocesan bishops continue to take a
lively interest in these matters once they have returned to
their sees or whether they will be content with having
won a paper victory and in fact allow control to slip back
into the hands of the curia. The pope's closing speeches
at this session were very noncommittal on such future
plans, although the appointment of two diocesan bishops,
Cardinal Lefebrve of Bruges and Cardinal Meyer of Chicago, to the Holy Office give reason to think that he intended something serious to be done. The death almost
immediately afterwards of Cardinal Meyer was a grave
blow to the Church.

Other propositions submitted to this session did not
meet with success. Most spectacular among the failures
was that on Missions, which in spite of a personal recom-
mendation by the pope was widely criticized by the bishops as being platitudinous and inadequate and was rejected by 1,601 votes to 311. A similar fate met the first
text of the propositions on Priestly Life and Service. There
is a critical situation, to be found in every country in the
world except perhaps in Ireland: there are not sufficient
priests offering themselves to fill the growing needs of the
world. What is the solution? Are we to recognize it as
a fact, whether edifying or not, that the presthood in the
past was to some extent recruited because a boy from a
poor family who went into the priesthood received an
education and perhaps a social position that he could not
hope to obtain if he remained in secular life and that, quite
apart from the question whether the age is becoming an
increasingly irreligious age, it was almost inevitable that a
desirable improvement in status of the layman both
in the religious and the secular world and a more ample
education would mean fewer recruits to the priesthood?
If so, was this merely to be accepted or was the problem to

be solved by ordaining deacons and by increasingly entrusting to laymen all tasks for which the priestly powers were not absolutely necessary? If so, in this new world what should be the relation and what the nature of authority between priest and layman?

These were intensely difficult but intensely important questions. It may be that they were not capable of neat answer in a document and that the answer could be discovered only by patience and experience in individual cases. But at any rate the criticism of the first draft presented to the Council was that it did not attempt to answer the questions or even to recognize their existence. It contented itself instead with pious platitudes. As such it was heavily criticized, defeated by a vote of 1,199 to 930, and sent back for rewriting. The propositions on the Renewal of the Religious Life also came under fire. Although it just managed to scrape a majority on most of its votes, it was not a two-thirds majority. The general demand was that the obligation of poverty should be accepted not only by the individual religious but by the religious house and the religious order. Not only monks but monasteries should be poor. There should be no grandiose buildings. It was agreed that new countries should be allowed to develop their own orders in accordance with their own circumstances and that small organizations with insufficient recruitment should be dissolved or amalgamated. Cardinal Spellman made an eloquent appeal warning the Fathers not to underestimate the contemplative life and saying that the Catholic world would be enormously impoverished by its disappearance. On the other hand, the propositions about the Formation of Priests was warmly welcomed. It was agreed that seminary education was at present too centrally regimented. The authority of Rome should be limited to a very general direction of the framework of the training. It was a matter in which local authorities should have wide autonomy to shape the courses in accordance with local customs. The seminarists should be less rigidly shut off from the secular world in which their pastoral life would subsequently be lived. Cardinal Léger bluntly denounced the phrase *philosophia perennis* as absurd and demanded its elimination. As yet, it must be confessed, the full measures of reform demanded here by the Council have not been introduced, but the burden of the Assembly's decree is very radical indeed.

Pius X in *Pascendi Gregis* had without equivocation stated that the scholastic philosophy was the teaching of the Church and that all instruction in seminaries was to take place in it. According to the demand of the Council all schools of thought and methods of approach must be fairly considered, each on its merits, and Thomism is no longer to be accorded a unique status. In a similar spirit, when the general question of Catholic education was considered, there was considerable criticism of the first proposed title on Catholic schools and it was agreed to drop it. Though bishops might state it as desirable that all Catholic children should be educated in Catholic schools, for one reason and another only some half of Catholic children in most countries are so educated. It was, argued many of the bishops, absurd to content oneself with a defeatist protest if children did not go to Catholic schools, to denounce all other schools as inevitably worldly, and unchristian to resign oneself to it that children who went to them were almost inevitably lost. In fact, while it is difficult in most countries to get exact statistics and would be difficult to interpret them even if one could get them, it appears that there is generally no enormously striking difference between the proportion that later abandon the faith among those who go and those who do not go to Catholic schools. It was, therefore, clearly a duty of ecclesiastical authorities not only to maintain Catholic schools but also to retain relations as friendly as possible with state schools—to see to it that in them proper facili-

ties for religious instruction and practice were provided
and that the general teaching was not vitiated by an anti-
Catholic bias.

The third session was mainly occupied with debates on
the relationship of the Church with the world—with the
draft on the Apostolate of the Laity and the so-called
schema XIII on the Church in the World Today, and the
declarations on non-Christians and on Religious Liberty,
but none of these was carried to a conclusion in this session. Yet what was notable about all these debates was
the emergence of a spirit of self-criticism, which was somewhat new in Catholic experience. Ever since the Reformation an all too common attitude of Catholic pronouncements had been that the Catholic Church was the Church
of Christ, that its message was offered to all men, and that
therefore all who were not Catholics were simply wrong
and to be condemned as such. If they had ever been members of the Church and had left it, they were deserving of
unqualified condemnation. Nothing but sheer wickedness
could explain such a preference for darkness to light. Just
as John XXIII had introduced into papal encyclicals a
habit of admitting a possibility that he might be wrong and
that different points of view might be possible, so the
Fathers at this Council showed themselves far more ready
to leave to God the task of passing judgement and to admit that whether one speaks of the troubles of the Reformation, of relations with other religions, or of the secular-
ism of the modern world, a large part of the responsibility
rests on the failure of Catholics. The Church would have
been less readily rejected if its message had been more
properly presented and if its members had shown themselves to the world as more worthy of their creed.

But there were some among the Fathers, just as there
were some in the world at large, who thought that the
majority of the bishops were carrying this process of self-
condemnation to a ridiculous and excessive pitch and

almost falling over themselves in ascribing to Catholics all the evils of the world. There was a reaction against self-condemnation.

The pope stood in a central position between these two groups. Critics from either side voiced their criticism— at least beneath their breath. Progressives alleged that he was not really in tune with the spirit of the age and did not wish to see the new reforms, whether in the liturgy or administration, become a reality. The conservatives announced that he had conceded too much. Time is still required before a final verdict can be passed, but it may well prove that there were extravagances on both sides that the pope in his central and balancing position did well to correct. It is certain that extreme conservatives who thought that nothing should be changed and that if the modern generation was deserting religion, all that was required was to denounce the modern generation were less than helpful.

It is equally certain that on the other side were to be found those who, proceeding from the very real need for certain reforms, had allowed themselves to fall into the habit of supporting every demand for reform that was put forward in the name of progress or democracy. Rightly calling for measures of decentralization, they were blind to the dangers of too indiscriminate a decentralization. Rightly noting the danger that came to the Church from excessive central power under Pius IX or Pius X, they did not sufficiently notice how the existence of such a power had saved the honour of the Church under Benedict XV, when all would certainly have been lost had there been no voice above that of national bishops. Whether the pope's tactics in detail were always the best is, of course, debatable. But his general purpose was clear. While in no way wishing to challenge the view that the Church was a sacramental body, a communion of the servants of Christ in which in that sense all were equal, or denying that that was its primary nature, yet they thought it necessary to insist that it had also a hierarchical nature. The Church did not solely nor even primarily consist of men in authority giving orders and men under authority accepting them. Anyone who depicted it as that alone gave an absurdly unbalanced picture. Yet it had its authoritarian nature. It had the power to bind and to loose, and the authority must be asserted—kept no doubt in reserve only to be used sparingly but nevertheless to be used in case of necessity. If it had not been that Pope John could speak to the world with an authority that no one else could command, the whole movement of the *aggiornamento* would never have got under way. The progressives would do themselves no service, saw Pope Paul, on the most pragmatic of planes if they diminished the authority that alone had and alone could have brought them to victory.

CHAPTER V

THE FOURTH SESSION

The fourth session was the session of decisions. Only the very important Schema XIII on the Church in the Modern World remained for debate in detail. All the rest were already in their final form, and it only remained to vote on them. Nobody wanted the Council to drag on any longer, so there was little desire to use procedural devices to re-open questions. The agenda passed through without substantial hitch, and all was voted as planned.

As they finally emerged, the Acts of the Council consisted of sixteen decrees, which can be divided into two classes. There were the decrees on the nature of the Church and the decrees on the nature of the World. The basic decree under the first heading was that on the Church, and subordinate to it were the decrees on Divine Revelation and on the Liturgy, on the Pastoral Office of the Bishops, on Missionary Activity, on the Eastern Catholic Church, on the Formation of Priests, on the Ministry and Life of the Priests, on the Adaptation and Renewal of Religious Life, on the Apostolate of the Laity, and on Christian Education. Under the second heading the basic decree was on the Church in the World Today, and subordinate to it were those on Ecumenism, on Mass Media, on Religious Liberty, and on Non-Christian Religions.

If one was to attempt to sum up the work of the Council in a single phrase, one might say that it was above all concerned with the nature of the Church. Its fundamental task was to correct the notion that the Church was primarily a hierarchical institution. It was indeed *incidentally* a hierarchical institution but only because it was *primarily* a sacrament of salvation. It was only after it had decided what its own nature was that the Church could fruitfully turn its attention to discussing its relation with other bodies outside itself—other Christian bodies, non-Christian religions, and the secular world. Thus it can be seen that the basic document of the Council is that on the Constitution of the Church. It is not an easy document and has been criticized both from the progressive and from the conservative side. But neither criticism is much justified. It is not a contradiction that the Constitution should insist both on the sacramental and on the authoritarian natures of the Church. For it has both natures, and it is essential to lay stress on both, just as it is essential to insist that Jesus Christ was both God and Man.

The liturgical reforms depend, of course, on the definition of the nature of the Church. The purpose of these reforms is to make the service of the Church as widely comprehensible as possible—hence the introduction of the vernacular—and to make the congregation as full participators in it as possible—hence the emphasis on dialogue, the Mass facing the people, and the like. Under the new dispensation there is to be more reading of the scriptures and more preaching. The criticism has been made that at the end of it all the liturgy remains to some extent remote from the people—indeed, making it word for word more intelligible has to some extent, we are told, only emphasized the more the difficulty of the whole service. But the criticism surely misses a point. The Mass celebrates, and indeed reenacts, the death for us of the Son of God. This is indeed a mystery, and no words or ritual can remove, or ought to try to remove, the mystery from it. All that the Church has a right to try to do is to make it as clear as possible to the people what the mystery is.

The decrees on missionary activity also logically followed the decree on the Constitution of the Church. If the Church was now to fulfil its duty of preaching to all nations in a fuller sense than it had ever done in the past, if the days of retreat into the catacombs were to be at an end, the missionary activity must necessarily be declared to be of the first importance. Yet the first of the drafts, though recommended by the pope, was, as I have said, considered by the Fathers to be pedestrian and uninspiring. The missionary bishops themselves did not want their work to be submitted to what was called a *Consilium Centrale Evangelisationis* to be established and to work out the policy after the Council was finished. They insisted on being given their marching orders here and now. Bishops at home like Cardinal Frings and Cardinal Bea gave them their support, and the first draft was rejected on November 9th, 1964 by 1,601 votes to 311. A central subcommission under Fr Johannes Schulte was then set up immediately, and a new draft was prepared and submitted to the fourth session in 1965 and passed. It was clear that the missionary bishops did not trust curial officials to have a proper understanding of their problems, which differed so widely from country to country. They wished central control to be as light as possible.

All were agreed on the importance of forming a native priesthood and handing authority over to it as soon as possible. No excuse must be given to Asian or African to believe that the Church was in any way the instrument of the white man's imperialism. The new attitude that refused to look on the pagans and non-Christians as in error and therefore to be denounced but looked for elements of goodness in their religions obviously required that the Church should be served in missionary countries only by priests very intimately acquainted with the details of the lives and religious practices of the natives. "These endeavours," said the decree, "need to be healed and illuminated, although by the gracious will of God in his providence, they can be sometimes considered as an education of the mind for the true God and a preparation for the Gospel." The "pilgrim Church" was "an envoy on the move." Many of the missionary bishops had asked for a clear definition to distinguish the notion of missionary work from general preaching activity, but the decree was not prepared to draw any hard and fast distinction. It merely replied to the demands of Cardinal Rugambwa and Archbishop Zoungrana that the missions were an essential and integral activity of the Church that will retain its importance "today and for ever." With the death of imperialism Christians must make themselves good citizens of their newly independent countries and share in the lives of those countries. "Christians are no different from other men in political and social institutions and in the language they speak."

Missionary activity in an ecumenically minded world poses certain problems that, it was alleged, the original decree passed over. It is a most common contention, the sense of which no one can fail to see, that one of the greatest obstacles to Christian missionary activity is that the Christian missionaries present themselves in the mission countries as rivals and belonging to different denominations. "How can we be expected to accept this Christianity," say the natives, "if the Christians cannot even agree among themselves what it says?" To meet this point non-Catholics in various places, as in South India, have in recent years attempted to present a united front. The Catholics, it was commonly said until recently, cannot of their nature cooperate in such an activity. The divine command, as they saw it, was that they should preach the Catholic faith and none other, whatever the inconveniences of doing so. Had ecumenical movements made it possible in any

way to modify this rigidity? Fr De Grijse, a missionary
superior-general, raised the point before the Assembly and
obtained the insertion of a section (section 6) that admitted the fact that the disunity among Christians in face
of the non-Christian was the greatest obstacle to missionary effort and demanded that Christians of the different
denominations should work together as much as possible.
It was not perhaps quite clear how close that cooperation
could be permitted to go. Obviously it could not go as far
as intercommunion such as is practised between certain
non-Catholic bodies, and obviously there is always a certain danger that a limited advance will only serve to emphasize the essential differences; and the situation of
course has its dangers because while on the one hand the
new freedom of communications makes more urgent than
before the need for missionary activity, on the other hand
the decay of religion and shortage of priests in many countries that had previously been called Catholic countries
naturally causes some at home to say, "To what purpose
is it for us to send our priests overseas when we so desperately need them here at home?"

The other main issue raised was that of the exact constitution of the congregation that was to take responsibility
for the Church's missionary activities in place of the now
abandoned *Consilium Centrale Evangelisationis*. It was
not possible to decide anything very definite until the general question of the future shape of Propaganda was decided. The Assembly eventually contented itself after
some debate with voting, "The bishops . . . advised by
the episcopal conferences . . . shall have an active part
with responsibility for decisions (*cum voto deliberativo*)
. . . in ways to be determined by the Roman Pontiff."

Out of the Constitution of the Church there flowed
necessarily certain institutional reforms. The pope of his
own motion promised the establishment of the new synod
of bishops, which had been so much talked about. No more

than fifteen percent of its members were to be papal nomi-
ness, the rest to be national representatives elected by
proportional representation. He also promised a reform of
the curia. How the reform of the curia will take place and
what exactly the synod of bishops will do is not as yet
quite clear. To some extent these problems will have to be
solved *ambulando*. Much depends on how strongly the
bishops' keenness for their synod is maintained or whether
with time the diocesans find themselves more interested
in the events of their sees than in what is going on at
Rome. At one time it had been thought that the synod
would be the body to whom would be entrusted the task of
seeing that the decisions of the Council were implemented, but this apparently is not to be so. The pope has
appointed a special post-conciliar central commission to
perform that duty.

The place of the episcopal conferences is more clearly
defined. Their functions are described in the decree on
the Pastoral Office of the Bishops. They are to be "the
common point where the bishops of a country or region
perform together their pastoral service to further the
higher good which the Church offers to mankind." These
conferences are to form their own constitutions subject to
the pope's approval. Their decrees will need a two-thirds
majority to be valid, but only under very special circumstances will they have the force of law. Christ entrusted
his commission to individuals—not merely to national
synods—and the Council has been too careful to free the
local bishop from too great a submission to Rome to submit him to a majority rule of the bishops of his own nation,
which might under certain circumstances prove a very
oppressive tyranny. Of course there is a certain air of compromise about such proposals. They offer a balance of
power, and, as is the case in all balances, occasional
tension is inevitable. It is both inevitable and, for all its
inconveniences, in the nature of the Church. The Cath-

olic way in this as in all matters is the middle way. The Church has always refused to say for the sake of simplicity either that all authority is at the centre or that there is no authority at the centre; it has rejected both Ultramontanism and Congregationalism. There is, let us confess, a certain small danger that the bishops might be tempted to ask too much for themselves. It was a little ominous that the very moderate proposal that a diocesan bishop should retire on a pension at seventy-five was dropped and that all that the Assembly would accept was a general exhortation to a bishop to retire when he found himself enfeebled by old age.

Underlying the whole work of the Council is, of course, the assumption and the hope that the new institutions will work because they will be infused by a new spirit. If men's minds remain merely authoritative—some thinking it their whole duty to give orders, others their whole duty merely to obey them—of course collegiality will become an empty and meaningless word. That is why the decree on the Life of the Priest is of the first importance. Its emphasis is on the priest's independence from the bishop and his need to collaborate with the laity. One of the major functions of the laity is to act as a bridge between the Church and the world. The Catholic layman is, of course, a full and equal member of the Church. The second chapter of the Constitution of the Church most fully recognizes that—more fully perhaps than the fourth chapter, which explicitly deals with the laity, or the decree on the Lay Apostolate. Yet the layman, fully a member of the Church, also belongs more fully to the world than can the cleric. He can exercise his lay apostolate—can work in the world for the glory of God. But he can do so only if he is allowed to work in reasonable freedom. Organized Catholic Action, working under the direct instruction of the bishop, is, of course, necessary on occasion. It has its place. But the sort of organization of Christian Democracy envisaged by Pius X when in *Pascendi Gregis* he ordered Catholics to submit their normal political conduct to the guidance of the bishop was, of course, a policy that in the modern world could only ensure that Catholic action be unsuccessful—partly because priests and bishops, not living in the world and not sharing the social and economic problems of the average man, are not likely to be good advisers on day-to-day policies and partly because, even if their advice was wise, a Catholic politician acting under the direct instruction of priests would be a suspect figure in the modern secular world.

The second central document of the Council was the Pastoral Constitution of the Church in the World Today, the so-called Schema XIII. At the fourth session all the other documents had already been debated. The Fathers had no duty left to them save to cast their votes. Schema XIII only remained to be debated, and the debates on it were the important debates of the Council's closing weeks. It was debated at great length, and there were five versions before the final form was approved. As was perhaps inevitable in a document in which so many hands had a part, there are certain verbal difficulties and ambiguities in it. Yet in general the document was welcomed as one of the most important of the Council, and when Cardinal Felici read out the figures of the final vote by which it was overwhelmingly passed, the Fathers broke out into loud applause in which the pope himself joined. He very largely repeated its argument in his own closing address to the Council on December 7th, 1965.

A footnote to the preface of the document explicitly explains that it is addressed to the whole world and not merely to the faithful. There is an *expositio introductiva,* which explains that it is the task of the Church to "read the signs of the times and to interpret them in the light of the Gospel." With that in view it then analyses the nature of the contemporary world as it sees it. It notes certain special marks of the age. Through scientific discovery the present age has won a command of the processes of nature incomparably greater than that of any of its predecessors. Such a command is in itself good and has made soluble many problems of economic production that were beyond the capacity of our ancestors. At the same time man has been terrified by some of his own discoveries. He has no longer the naïve confidence of the Victorians that his discoveries will all be inevitably beneficial. He is terrified at the increase in his own powers of destruction, and deeper knowledge has made him not more confident but "more uncertain of himself." Many find it hard "to recognize the eternal values and to harmonize them with the challenge of new factors." Improvements in communications have made the human race more evidently a unity, involved in one single fate of good or ill, than ever before.

In the first chapter of the first main section the Constitution describes the Christian view of man with his double nature, born to serve God and yet with his vision of God obscured by the barriers of original sin. Man can neither escape from his belief in God nor see God clearly face to face. In the mysterious purposes of Providence, God is a reality but at the same time a hidden God—a *Deus absconditus*. From Man's interdependence the Constitution deduces the need for his "socialization." It was in Leo XIII's time that the Church first considered the problems created by the new industrialism, but the social encyclicals of Leo XIII and Pius XII—*Rerum Novarum* and *Quadragesimo Anno*—great documents though they were, were both essentially national documents. They explained how property and power and wealth should be distributed within a particular nation, but they took it for granted that the economic unit was the single nation. They had nothing to say about how far it was just that there should be widely different standards between different countries and continents nor, if just at all, what were the criteria of this international justice. Perhaps communications in those earlier years were still so uncertain that there was no practical alternative but to accept the differences as facts. In any case, the earlier popes did so accept them.

It was the special achievement of John XXIII in *Mater et Magistra* and *Pacem in Terris* to insist that there was an obligation of international social justice as well as of national social justice—to insist that it was the duty of the Catholic in a developed country to work for the raising of the standards of the underdeveloped countries and that we could not say that social justice had been achieved until the intolerably wide gap between the two sets of societies had been abolished or at least narrowed. At the moment, so far from that gap narrowing, there was some reason to think that it was widening—that the standards in the developed countries were increasing very rapidly, those in the underdeveloped countries a great deal less rapidly, and the gap between the two increasing. The Constitution underlined Pope John's words and insisted that our social duty was to all men not merely to Catholics.

The fourth chapter is the central chapter of the Constitution. It insists on the Catholic's duty to humanize all personal relations everywhere in the world—to leaven the whole lump. "Let its radiance flow out over the whole world." It can do so primarily by reminding man of the meaning of his existence as the creature of God. The Catholic must play his full part in all legitimate secular organizations of his society. The Constitution praises the "other Christian churches" for all "their common effort in the fulfilment of this task." The people of God, it says, must "listen carefully to the various tongues in which the world speaks today. They must learn to understand and interpret them in the light of the divine word, so that divine truth may be better perceived and grasped, and so propounded more aptly." By this text, the final draft of

which was mainly the work of the French Dominican Fr
Chenu, the old conception of a Church on the retreat,
protecting itself against the assaults of a wicked and godless world, was finally repudiated. The Church was the
inheritor of the Gospel, which was to be preached to all
men. It was its duty, as Newman put it, to go forth "con-
quering and to conquer."

But of course Catholics being called on to work in the
world and being forbidden to turn away from it as an im-
possibly evil place did not mean that the Fathers fatuously
suggested that all was right with the world. On the contrary, before they came to any particular problems, they
first noted the prevalence of atheism on a scale more wide-
spread than had probably ever before been known. It was
well for the Fathers to dedicate themselves and to bid
Catholics to dedicate themselves to the task of reminding
man that he was the creature of God. Yet many millions
and many who gave their minds to the social problems of
the day had no conception of themselves as being of such a
nature. On the contrary, the introduction of God into the
consideration of such problems seemed to them the introduction of a supreme irrelevance.

When the matter was first discussed at the second debate on the Constitution, a number of speeches—by the
Patriarch Maximos, by Archbishop Seper, by Fr Arrupe,
the Jesuit General, by Cardinal Konig and others—criticized the language in which God's relevance was asserted
as unconvincing. Four hundred and fifty Fathers, it is said,
had sent in a petition asking for a specific condemnation
of atheistic Communism. The majority were opposed and
thought that such a condemnation by name would destroy
the whole virtue of the approach. The great defect of
modern society was its loss of faith in a God who really
acted in the world. People took it for granted that his intervention in the affairs of the world was unthinkable. It is
true, of course, that Marxian Communists made their

repudiation of God explicit and defiant. But it would be a great mistake to allow it to appear that all who happened to be opposed to Communism were therefore automatically defenders of Christianity and entitled to be hailed as its champions. On the contrary, much that was done in the way of anti-Communism was, whether it proclaimed itself as atheist or not, obviously entirely irreligious. The Constitution, referring to such encyclicals as *Divini Redemptoris, Apostolorum Principes, Mater et Magistra* and *Ecclesiam Suam* without mentioning Communism by name, condemns indeed "baneful activities" that the Church "cannot but firmly condemn as it has done in the past," but its main concern is with inquiring how it happens that so many men, created in the image of God and possessed of a nature born for the belief in God, nevertheless come to repudiate him. The great need, it decides, is not to turn outward and denounce other people but for Catholics to turn inward and to ask themselves how far their own failures of conduct or false presentation of their faith may be responsible for their neighbours' atheism.

The two great problems on which the world was most insistently calling for a pronouncement from the Church are certainly birth control and nuclear warfare. If it cannot find anything clear to say on these great questions, says the man in the street, it cannot expect to be taken seriously as the world's teacher. It is not an unreasonable demand.

On marriage and the family there is a great distinction between the Church's teaching on divorce and that on birth control. The secular world does not insist on absolutely indissoluble marriage. It allows divorce for various causes, but it recognizes that divorce, even if sometimes a necessary evil, is nevertheless an evil. The ideal it recognizes is that marriage should be lasting and satisfactory, so even if he is not able to agree with it entirely, the secularist does not quarrel with the Church when it bids husbands and wives to be faithful to one another and to act responsibly for the sake of the children. It agrees that it is better for people to behave in such a way even if they think that it is asking too much to expect that they will always do so. Sensible secularists had no wish to argue that an arrangement of total licence was an arrangement that would be likely to make for human happiness. Marriage was admitted to be an arrangement that made for happiness on the most secular principles. The secularists only asked that a remedy be provided for the unfortunate cases when it has in fact broken down.

Birth control was a different matter. A large number of secularists believed that the increase of population was one of the great problems and one of the great evils of the day. Population, thanks to the great and desirable decrease in infant mortality, was increasing with unprecedented rapidity—increasing so rapidly as virtually to eat up any increase in productivity and to threaten mankind with the menace of a population explosion. There was, it was urged, a demographic problem. Side by side with it was a personal problem. The old view that the sole proper purpose of copulation was procreation was, it was argued, manifestly inadequate. Abstinence between married people was not desirable and might well threaten the companionship of marriage. It was an evil—or in many cases might be an evil. Copulation might be more satisfactory when it was undertaken with a readiness to accept children if children should come. The Church might well be right in telling people that they did wrong and did themselves an injury if they did not set out to have a reasonable family. But there were circumstances when for medical or for economic reasons it was not possible, for the moment or permanently as the case might be, for the mother to have another baby. It was desirable to have a reasonable family. But it was also desirable—or often

desirable—to space out the children. The question was
not, Should parents use contraceptives irresponsibly and
indiscriminately? but, What should they do when it was
not possible at the moment to have another child? The
safe period might be a sufficient answer when it was
merely inconvenient to have a child. Then it might be
possible to take a certain chance. But when it was medi-
cally impossible to have a child, the safe period was manifestly insufficient. By its advocacy of spacing, by its admission that there were times when it was both permitted
and desirable to use the safe period, the Church had admitted the desirability of planned families. Was there any
valid distinction between the method of the safe period
and the method of the contraceptive?

This is not the place to attempt to answer these questions. All that it is necessary to say is that all the world
knows that they are the kinds of questions that are most
frequently being asked throughout the whole secular and
the whole Catholic world today, and they were asked as
insistently in the Vatican Council as anywhere else. There
was a fundamental difference between the secularist's
attitude toward the Church's teaching on marriage and his
attitude toward the Church's teaching on contraception.
On marriage the secularist thought that the Church was
teaching a high ideal and only in error only insofar as it
was asking of human nature more than human nature was
capable. On birth control the secularist thought that the
Church was insisting on a teaching that was antisocial
and a danger to the race. Unbridled increase in population was, it was said, the main cause of war, and the
Church was propagating a doctrine that could lead to a
world war. What was the authority on which the Church
based itself in its condemnation of contraception? Was
there any chance that the teaching would be modified?

These, as we know, are some of the most debated questions of the day. Contraception is the issue on which the

teaching of the Church is in most definite conflict with the teaching of the modern secular world. It might have seemed reasonable that a document descriptive of the Church and the Modern World would tell us the Church's teaching on this point. But the pope decided that the issue was so crucial that he must take the matter into his own hands. He set up a special commission to advise him, and when that commission failed to reach agreement, he remitted the matter to another commission. That second commission has recently reported to him, and he will in due course give his own ruling; but whatever he says, the manoeuvres and the debates have in themselves profoundly changed the situation. Twenty years ago couples were forbidden the use of contraceptives, being told, whether they understood the reasoning or not, that the Church's teaching on the matter was certain. But it is one thing to ask the faithful to obey what they believe to be the certain mind of the Church. It is quite another to ask them to obey a ruling that is clearly so uncertain that both bishops and experts are to be found on both sides.

That there was difference of opinion on the question the debates in the Council very sufficiently proved. There was indeed a conservative school that did not hide its regret that the matter had ever been raised at all. Cardinal Ruffini expressed this point of view very strongly. Other Fathers criticized what they called "situation ethics." Cardinal Heenan criticised the *periti* who had collaborated in producing the schema and demanded that the faithful should at least be given clear rulings so that couples could know for certain what they were and were not allowed to do. Cardinal Ottaviani wanted the regulation of families to be left exclusively to Providence. But Cardinal Alfrink, Patriarch Maximos, and Bishop Reuss, speaking explicitly in the name of 124 bishops from various countries, demanded an examination of the traditional teaching about methods. They affirmed without qualification the necessity of limiting the number of children and asserted that there was at least a *dubium honestum* about the methods of limitation that might be judged legitimate. The Fathers did not to any important extent think it within their terms of reference to talk about the "pill" in particular. They were more concerned with the general problem of definition of the conduct that was required for the preservation of a full married life in which the sexual act had a purpose far beyond that of mere reproduction. Their hope was, as Patriarch Maximos put it, to bridge "the discrepancy between the official doctrine of the Church and the contrary practice of the immense majority of Christian couples."

As for the actual phraseology of the Constitution, in this matter it was much less outspoken in the end than had been the debates in the Assembly. Warned not to give any rulings by the pope's instructions, the Assembly contented itself with asserting that the faithful were forbidden the use of methods considered unlawful by the *magisterium,* which of course was true enough, but the question what methods were considered lawful was just the question in debate.

The other challenge was the challenge of the new nuclear weapons. The words of Christ and the principles of the Christian religion make it inevitable that war should be an exercise uniquely hateful to the Church. The early Christians were a minute and uninfluential minority. Their influence over imperial policy did not require them to bother themselves with the question whether the State had a right to employ military force, but with the establishment of a nominally Christian society that question had to be faced. The general mind of the Church did not accept a doctrine of full and unconditioned pacifism. To command nonresistance without qualification and under all circumstances was, it was thought, to oversimplify the problem. There were times when it appeared a Christian duty to

defend if not oneself, at any rate one's neighbours or one's
dependents. There were times when the use of a little
violence now might prevent greater violence in the end.
Therefore, while those who chose the way of pacifism
were in no way condemned, the Church has never imposed
such a doctrine as obligatory. On the other hand, it has always preached that war is a very great evil that can be justified only if certain rigid conditions are present. Whether
through the centuries Christians have paid as much attention to these conditions in practice as they should have is
problematical. But certainly the last three popes have
shown again and again that they see the problem of world
peace as the greatest of all the secular problems of the
world. Their task has not been a simple one.

For the Church is committed not only to the cause of
peace but also to the cause of justice, and the First World
War left in power in Russia a regime that many people
with a good deal of reason saw as the implacable enemy
both of religion and of good living. Was it possible to make
peace with a Communist regime? Or, if it was necessary
to insist that a worthy peace could only be established
through resistance to Communism, did not that mean that
although the Church might advocate peace as the final
object, in practise and in the world as it was it was asserting
that peace could be attained only as the result of war?
Similar dilemmas were set by the establishment of a regime at least as evil in Nazi Germany.

Whatever the correct attitude toward these difficult
problems, Pope John XXIII thought that there was nothing to be gained by a refusal to accept the fact that Communist regimes were in power in Eastern European countries. The Church must not in any way abate its hostility
to the principles of Marxian Communism. But a man was
more than a theory. People were not wholly the creatures
of their principles—sometimes for the worse and sometimes for the better. Individual Communists, however mis-

guided their principles in general, were not necessarily incapable of a good action in particular. In any event, there was no sane alternative to trying to establish some *modus vivendi* with them and trying to find a means of breaking the vicious circle of the international arms race.

It is the new weapons that have given their new dimension to the problem of war. When our ancestors thought of war, they thought of an army standing along the frontier and repelling the invader and thus saving the people of the interior from the devastation of war. It was easy enough in such circumstances to assert that a nation had the right to defend itself but not the right to attack, that it was legitimate to kill the soldiers who were attacking your country but not to kill civilians. But in this modern world of nuclear weapons and total war what pertinence had such principles? How could a nation defend itself except by attacking from the air or through guided missiles miles behind the enemy's frontiers? How was it possible to prevent such attacks from incidentally killing many civilians? Indeed, since under totalitarian organization the civilians were assisting the war effort just as much as the soldiers in uniform, what was the moral principle that validly commanded that only those in uniform should be attacked? The traditional conditions required for a just war hardly applied to a world of totalitarian war. They were adumbrated for a society that presumed that its wars would be limited. But what was the conclusion to be drawn from that? Was the conclusion that the traditional principle of a just war was irrelevant to the modern total world? Or was it rather that since total wars could not of their nature be fought without violating the traditional principles, they were therefore of their nature immoral? Or is some middle course, some restatement of the traditional teaching in a form that would make it meaningful in the modern world still possible?

The majority of bishops come, of course, from uncom-

mitted countries that do not themselves possess nuclear
weapons. It was, therefore, natural enough that their in-
stinct should be to vote for the total abolition of nuclear
weapons. But a mere vote in favour of total disarmament
obviously did not in itself get things very much further.
How could the bishops—or anybody else—persuade the
citizens and governments of the heavily armed countries—
Russia and America—to disarm? They could issue pious
appeals. Could they do more? Would they be justified in
saying that the possession of nuclear weapons was immoral
and that therefore—it was to be presumed—anyone who
served in an army that was dependent on or prepared to
use nuclear weapons was committing a mortal sin? In fact,
if such a pronouncement were to be issued, very many
American Catholics would clearly pay no attention to it.
A few might obey. There might be a certain increase in
American conscientious objectors. It is not to be believed
that anyone in Russia would pay any attention. The Rus-
sian people would probably never even hear of such a ruling. Therefore the effect, if there was to be any effect at all,
would probably be somewhat to lessen the American military potential to the advantage of the Russians. Would
that be fair or desirable? And as for the disarmers in the
uncommitted countries—were they really the moral su-
periors of the Americans? Or was it rather true that they
piously voted for their resolutions for the abolition of
nuclear weapons, comfortably conscious that the Americans in fact possessed such weapons and had no intention
of abandoning them and that therefore they were running
no real risk by their gesture?

Again, is it intrinsically wrong to threaten to use these
nuclear weapons? Or is it only wrong for one nation to
threaten to use them against another? If an effective
world authority, for which both Pope John and Pope Paul
had so cogently pleaded, should come into existence,
would it be permissible for the world authority to equip

itself with such weapons? Was there any validity in the contention that one could not condemn the nuclear weapons as such since there was at least a theoretical possibility that they would be used in a legitimate way—such as against a fleet at sea, where their use would not involve the destruction of civilian lives nor have incalculable after effects? Or ought one rather to face the fact that the overwhelming probability is that if these weapons are used at all, they will be used illegitimately—that all the nations have indeed confessed to strategic plans that Catholic teaching most plainly forbids? And that therefore it is sophistry to allow those nations to keep their weapons on the plea that it is just possible to think up some highly improbable hypothetical circumstance when they might be used legitimately?

In his address to the World Medical Association on September 30th, 1954, Pope Pius XII spoke with as little equivocation as could be imagined: "If despite these efforts the setting in motion of an ABC (atomic, bacteriological and chemical) war meant that it would bring in its wake such widely spread evil effects as were completely beyond human control, then its use would have to be rejected as immoral, for it would then be a case not just of defense against injustice but of an annihilation of all human life within the radius of the destructive action, which was not permissible on any account." John XXIII said in *Pacem in Terris* that in modern circumstances it was almost impossible to think of a war that would be a just war. "In this age which boasts of its atomic power it no longer makes sense to maintain that war is a fit instrument with which to repair the violation of justice." It was thus difficult for the Fathers to know exactly what to say. But in face of the pope's pronouncements, of Christ's and the Church's teaching, and of the agony of the world, they would clearly have made themselves a laughing stock had they said nothing.

The text of the relevant chapter—chapter five—on Peace and the Fellowship of Nations as originally presented was almost unequivocally pacifist. It condemned the use of nuclear weapons and all nuclear stockpiling. This first wording was vigorously attacked by such Americans as Archbishop Hannan and Cardinal Spellman, who argued that the document as presented was manifestly unfair. It condemned those who had possessed themselves of these weapons as weapons of defence and by doing so had preserved peace and the democratic life. What is defence and what is offence is, as Talleyrand found with treason, to some extent a matter of dates; and as a matter of historical fact the most striking advantages of Communism —the seizure by Communist regimes of the countries of Eastern Europe and of China—had all taken place at a time when the Americans alone had nuclear weapons. It was most doubtful how far such weapons were used or could ever be used in practice to check aggression. It was quite arguable that they were in fact so horribly unusable that the possession of them was rather a weakness than a strength. They inhibited even the use of other weapons because of the ever constant fear that even a limited war would in fact escalate into a nuclear war.

But whatever the truth about such arguments, it had to be admitted that the argument in favour of nuclear weapons in the hands of the unaggressive as a guarantor of peace, if not wholly valid, was at least not so plainly invalid as to make it just to declare anyone who believed it or acted on it to be in mortal sin. For the Church, it must always be remembered, is in these matters not so much concerned with what policy should ideally be advocated as with what policy is so utterly evil as to be declared without equivocation to be a sin. Yet if the possession of nuclear weapons was not to be condemned, what could the Assembly say that was of any use at all? It was said that the Americans did not intend to wish to use these weapons. No one supposes that anyone but a lunatic intends to use them. But when the argument goes forward from that to assert, "We hold these weapons not to attack others but only to deter others from attacking us," the ominous comment is that they can be effective only as a deterent if the possessor of them is prepared to use them, or at least has persuaded his antagonist that he is prepared to use them under certain circumstances. If they are never to be used, they are merely expensive bluff. And in view of the Catholic tradition and Pius XII's words were the Fathers prepared to condone their use even if only in retaliation?

Quite frankly, it is not clear from the document. The Fathers did not hesitate—it could hardly be expected that they would—to make clear their horror of war. The monstrous perils of an armaments race are vividly described. The statesmen of the world are warned that in a world where the ultimate weapons are nuclear, there is a grave danger even in the accumulation of the conventional weapons. Armaments, the world was told, were "one of the gravest scourges of mankind" and "an intolerable injury to the poor." Out of deference to American protests the phrase "balance of terror" was omitted from the final text, but the intention of condemnation was clear enough. The rights of the conscientious objector, about which the Church, for all Benedict XV's condemnation of war and of conscription, had been so incomprehensibly reticent, was at last unequivocally affirmed. Total war was condemned without reserve, as was any warlike action that involved the destruction of whole cities and their inhabitants. It might be argued that any modern war was so certain to become a total war and to involve such indiscriminate destruction that such proclamations logically involved an absolute renunciation of war. But the Fathers did not draw such a conclusion. They called for the establishment of a world authority, but until such an authority was established, they specifically asserted that a government "when all the resources of peaceful negotiations have been exhausted" had the right to defend itself—though not to use forbidden means to do so even if its opponent used them.

The cynic might say that the Constitution said that the Catholic was allowed to fight a war but he was on no account allowed to win it, and it can hardly be denied that there are some verbal confusions in the document. This arises from the fact that it was an attempt to reconcile wide differences between the American bishops and those from other countries. Even the tentative approaches to pacifism that the document took were a shock to many of them, and the *modi* on pacifism, though carried, were not carried by the overwhelming majorities that were common in votes on clauses of this Constitution and on other subjects. Four hundred and eighty-three votes were cast against them.

When ecclesiastical documents, whether they be papal encyclicals, bishops' pastorals, or decrees of the Council, are engaged in laying down liturgical regulations or rules of discipline for the faithful, they tend to be very exact. Critics have sometimes complained of them for being too meticulous. But when the pope or the Council speaks on a political or social problem and to the whole world, there is no alternative but to speak in more general terms. The danger with such documents is not that either the faithful or the world at large will contradict such pronouncements but rather that they will pay no attention to them. The documents themselves are issued in a hope that they may play their part in giving the world a general guidance toward better things but with no expectation that they will, like some rule of discipline, be immediately accepted by the whole world. Thus freed from danger of contradiction and of challenge by the acid test of actuality, their authors are tempted sometimes to side-step difficulties by allowing contradictions to go unresolved. Thus in his great encyclical *Rerum Novarum* Leo XIII argued on the one hand that property should be widely distributed so that as nearly as possible every family might have its share of it. On the other hand, he said that the existing rights of property were sacrosanct and any attack on them was forbidden. In a new country, where there was plenty of unoccupied land, it was easy enough to see how some could be given more without others having to have less. In a fully settled country it was not easy to see how this could be done. The Council to some extent left a similar confusion about its attitude toward war.

It is clear enough from the pronouncements of Pius XII, John XXIII, and Paul VI that the papal attitude is that not only is war a gigantic evil but that under modern conditions it is very unlikely to be waged by means that Catholic teaching could find permissible. Therefore the popes have no hesitation in supporting all policies designed to prevent war—disarmament, world authorities, and the like—nor had the Council any hesitation in following them in such support. One can hardly doubt that in almost any conceivable circumstances that might arise, they would counsel the acceptance even of onerous conditions as a lesser evil than war. But is it possible for them to impose on the Catholic world an obligation of absolute and unconditioned pacifism—to command unilateral disarmament if multilateral disarmament should not be possible? Could they feel justified in saying that anyone who serves in the armed forces of a modern state is in mortal sin? They were not prepared to go as far as that. They were only prepared to assert the right of a conscientious objector to refuse to serve. Even such an assertion was a novelty.

The Council's decree is not, then, a declaration of absolute pacifism. But it is a step in that direction. In the eighteenth and nineteenth centuries popes said nothing to challenge the common belief that the canon was the *ultima ratio regum;* nor did they dispute it that war, though it was a great evil, did in itself settle things. The invader was driven back, the country remained free. It is clear to popes and Councils—as indeed to other people—that under modern conditions war is not only inexpressibly horrible but also senseless. To attack one's enemies with hydrogen bombs cannot except by the greatest violence to language be called an exercise in self defence; nor is it possible to fight against an enemy who is armed with such weapons except by the use of such weapons. Therefore, it is necessary to find a way of abolishing war altogether. For war no longer, as in the past, leads to victory. As President Kennedy said, "If we do not end war, war will end us."

Pius XII bade us be prepared to suffer a good deal of injustice rather than plunge the world into war. No sane man can quarrel with that. No sane man can doubt that many—probably most—of the wars of history have been between rulers who did not differ so radically from one another that the transfer of some territory from one power to another was a far lesser evil than the evil of a world war. Who could really deny that the differences in moral standards of the German and the Allied Governments in 1914 were not sufficient to justify a world war of such appalling dimensions and that it was not worth while drenching the world in blood to decide whether Alsace should be ruled by France or Germany? It is not so easy to pass a verdict of that sort on the Second World War. Was Hitler a uniquely evil man—a man so evil that it was worth while even having a world war to rid ourselves of him? If we had let him have his way, what would have been the outcome? There would doubtless have been unspeakable atrocities for the immediate future. But before very long Hitler would have died. Would the German nation have sickened of atrocity and returned to more normal habits? It is, of course, true that such a return to normality would have taken place only after many men and women had suffered unjustly. Their suffering would indeed have been a grave evil, but would it have been a greater evil than the evil of World War II? Who shall evaluate? All that it is relevant to say here is that the Council and the Church through the Council have not on this, as on many other points, told us with simple clarity what answer to give; they have seen it rather as their task to tell us what question to ask. The document concedes the right of "legitimate defence" but does not define what constitutes legitimate defence. It is an important document but essentially a document of transition. Further work has still to be done before it can be said that the Church has in any way a final and definite view on these matters.

CHAPTER VI

THE EFFECT

The Council, said Pope Paul in his closing address on December 8th, 1965, has been "one of the greatest events in the history of the Church." For four hundred years the Church had been an army on the defensive. Attacked first by positive Protestantism and afterwards by infidelity, the ecclesiastical authorities had thought, naturally enough, that their first task was to prevent the disruption of Christendom in Europe and to defend the faithful against its attacks. After four centuries it had to be recognized that Catholic unity in that old sense had irrevocably perished. There was no chance that Protestant bodies would prove to be but temporary aberrations and that the people of those countries would return to their medieval uniformity. There was equally no chance that the challenges of modern invention and modern thought would be easily refuted by the quotation of a few sentences from St Thomas Aquinas. On the other hand, while the day of Catholic countries as such had passed, the intermixture of peoples and the improvement of communications offered to Catholicism an opportunity to make its message a worldwide message to a degree that it had never previously been and imposed upon the Church an obligation to restate its teaching in a way that would make it appear relevant to modern man and his problems. Of course, as with all the great turning events of history, this was an event that did not suddenly and unexpectedly emerge out of a clear sky on one particular day. Things happen like that in plays or novels but not in reality.

From Leo XIII's time onwards—to go no further back —the Church had been steadily moving toward an adjustment of its message in order to make it relevant to the age. It was not so much a question of whether new methods of expression and practice were intrinsically better than the old as that the new methods of expression were required if the new age was to attend to them. Truth, like justice, must not only be true but must be seen to be true. After the Council is finished, much still remains to be done before we can confidently say that its decisions represent a really new approach rather than paper resolutions that merely make a pretence that something will be done. The summer of 1966 was in Rome in the fashion of that climate the period of *vacatio legum,* and in September a theologian's conference under Fr Dhanis, S.J., met at the Gregorian University to consider the detailed methods of the implementation of the decrees. Those who have read through the decrees and the reports about them have now had the opportunity of beginning to judge how successfully and with what vigour the decrees of the Council are being actually put into practice. Will the synod of bishops, for instance, be a reality or a mere formality? The formal announcement of its formation gives no answer to that question. Only the event can provide the answer.

The First Vatican Council, the Council of Trent, and the medieval Councils were General Councils in theory, but in their personnel they were only Councils of Europeans. The early Councils of the Church were in personnel indeed more Greek than Latin, but they were not for that reason less limited. The Second Vatican Council assembled Fathers of every nationality and from every corner of the world on a scale that had never before been approximated. It is the first General Council that has really been general. It is only in these last years that a pope speaking *urbi et orbi* has really spoken to the whole world and not merely to the Roman world. Previous generations were not necessarily to blame for this defect, for it was circumstances rather than their own lack of faith that prevented them. But it is only in our time and only with the Second Vatican Council that the Church has begun a serious coordinated attempt to "go out and teach all nations"—literally *all* nations. We stand, whether we like it or not, at the threshold of a great era, offering great opportunities and, as opportunities always do, carrying with it great dangers.

Pope John XXIII summoned the Council, as he explained, not to denounce and condemn dangerous heresies but to renew the life of the Church, to remove from the practice of all Catholics any obstacle that might be an unnecessary barrier to the acceptance of the Church by those living outside it. The first step that proved that the Fathers were determined to take this invitation seriously and had no intention of being treated like rubber stamps to give automatic approval to proposals previously drafted and presented to them in cut and dried form was their refusal on the Council's first day to accept without question the personnel of the preparatory commissions laid before them and their insistence on making a real choice for themselves. The basic lines of the real programme were laid down in the first discussion on the schema on the Church, and these were summarized by Pope Paul VI in his opening address to the second session. They were a deepening of the self-consciousness of the Church, inner reform, ecumenical discussion, and the dialogue with the world.

The freedom of speech that was insisted upon by Pope John and which was in some ways in marked contrast with the manners that reigned at the First Vatican Council, was far more than a mere evidence of good will and good faith. It introduced a habit of freedom into the Church's life that will in many ways probably prove at least as important as any of its concrete decisions. One sometimes comes across disgruntled critics of the Council who say that such freedom of speech was indeed permitted so long as the Council was in session and until decisions were taken but that, the decisions taken, we need not expect that people will be allowed to go on debating them as if the matters were still open. But in reality a new habit has been created. The spirit has escaped from the box, and it is highly improbable that it will ever again be possible to get it back in again, even if anyone should be so misguided as to try. Freedom can be wholly suppressed only where there is a people who take its absence for granted and who do not expect to be allowed to speak freely. But it is likely that in the perspective of time, if the result of the Council is a great extension of freedom, then, while history will continue to pay its full tribute to Pope John, there will also be a wider understanding than is sometimes found today of the contribution to it of Pope Paul. For Pope Paul, accepting the protest against the tyranny of a minority over a majority, has also been careful to prevent that more subtle and hardly less dangerous tyranny of a majority over a minority.

In fact one of the outstanding successes of the Council was in the ecumenical field. The differences between the denominations have not, of course, been utterly abolished. What sane man could have expected that they would be? But a man of middle age cannot but fail to note the quite extraordinary change in the attitude of Christian to Christian today from that of his boyhood. The rudeness with which religious arguments were usually carried on a generation ago seems to us today something quite extraordinary. The growth in the dialogue of courtesy has been remarkable and utterly welcome. Of course, the changes here cannot, any more than the changes in other fields,

be put down entirely to the Council. The Council built on
conditions that had already been created. What else could
it have done? It could not have carried through policies
that had been utterly undreamed of before it met. In the
Nazi concentration camps Catholics and Protestants had
suffered together and had learned in suffering how much
they had in common. The previous Archbishop of Canterbury had already paid his visit to Pius XII. A spirit was
abroad in the world. Still, that spirit might have been rebuked. It was instead encouraged. Whereas so often in the
past theologians had been anxious to emphasize the differences between Catholics and those of other denominations, now they were anxious rather to dwell on the beliefs
that Catholics had in common with other Christians and
with non-Christians—the common belief in God with the
other religions, the common belief in Christ and the bond
of baptism with other Christians. Emphasis was laid on
the great tasks the men of all religions must perform together if the world was to be saved.

If one tried to sum up the achievement of the Council,
it would be possible to do so perhaps under the following
headings.

First, there was the return to the Bible. A consequence
of the sixteenth-century Protestant appeal to the uninter-
preted Bible was that post-Reformation Catholics tended
to turn away from the Bible—in practice often to neglect
it—in a way that the pre-Reformation Catholic had never
done. The modern Catholic was told that the Church was
the source of authority and often almost believed that it
really would have hardly mattered whether the Bible had
been written or not. Although Catholics hotly repelled the
charge when they were told by Protestant critics that they
were not allowed to read the Bible, all too few of them did
in fact read it, and all too many more were grossly ignorant
of it. The Council did well when it insisted that the Bible
as well as tradition was a source of revelation and author-

ity for the Catholic. By doing so it made easier the possibilities of dialogue with the Protestants. It did not cure all differences between Catholic and Protestant, but at least it ensured that when they talked together, they did not talk from wholly different premises.

Not only did the Council bid Catholics go back to the Bible, but it also bade them go back to it in a much more enlightened spirit than that of the past. If not exactly a document of the Council, at least there was a document issued during the Council—the instruction of the Biblical Commission of April 21st, 1964—that marked, we may say, the final death of the view that Catholics were committed to any theory of literal verbal inspiration of the Scriptures. Such teaching was not new. The Biblical Commission was substantially repeating what had already been said by Pius XII, just as Pius in his time was repeating what had been said before him by Leo XIII. It said that the principles of hermeneutics must be applied to all the Bible—to the New Testament as much as to the Old—and it insisted that the Gospels were concerned with "preaching" the lessons of Christ, not merely with "memorizing" his words.

In the nineteenth century both Catholics and Protestants were in considerable confusion about what they were supposed to believe about the Bible. In both camps there were to be found many who thought themselves obligated to give a literal assent to every apparently historical statement of the Bible and hence to deny the new claims that were being made by biologists and geologists. Such fundamentalists are still to be found, and there has been a strange revival of fundamentalism in quite sophisticated university circles. But it is no longer a position held by the leaders of Protestant denominations, and by making it clear that it is not imposed on Catholics, the Council has certainly removed one of the obstacles to ecumenical dialogue. But there is all the difference between

belief in the historical validity of the Pentateuch and belief in the historical validity of the Resurrection. The
Catholic way is, as always, the middle way.

The Church cannot admit, and the Council does not
admit, any compromise on the creeds, and the condemnation of modernist extravagances still stands. The Council
did not consider it within its terms of reference to lay
down the details of hermeneutic principles. It was only
concerned with proclaiming the proper rights of scholarship to whatever conclusion they might lead the scholar.
The liturgical reforms insisted on a more prominent part
for readings from scripture in the Church's services than in
the past and that those readings be in the vernacular language and hence intelligible to the ordinary member of a
congregation.

Second, the Council has definitely committed the
Church to the acceptance of Newman's doctrine of development. As Cardinal Gracias of India put it, Newman's
doctrine of development was the testing ground of all the
deliberations of the Council—a book, it is amusing to notice, the greater part of which was written when Newman
was still an Anglican. When Newman's doctrine was
launched a century and a quarter ago into the static Catholic world of that day, there were many—most notably perhaps Orestes Brownson in America—who thought of it
as the new and very dangerous doctrine of a recent con-
vert who had by no means fully thrown over the Protestantism in which he had been raised. A common view of
those times was that the Christian faith had been delivered to the Church once and for all and that when faced
with modern assertions that were not contained in it the
Church had no task except to declare its opposition. Newman reminded the Catholic world that Christ not only
revealed his truth to mankind but also left behind him the
Comforter to be with the Church and to lead it into all
truth. It was reasonable that modern discoveries should

not be faced with a blank negative but that there should be a defining voice that could determine how the ancient teaching could be expressed in terms of the new problem. As John XXIII put it in his inaugural address to the Council, "The authentic doctrine should be studied and expounded through the literary forms of modern thought. One thing is the ancient doctrine of the *depositum fidei* and another is the way in which it is presented."

The Church claims no right to invent doctrines hitherto unheard of. That would have been an intolerable claim on any Christian principles. But it claims a right to develop traditional Christian doctrine in order that it might provide its new definition of old principles to meet the challenges of the day. Although Newman's theory of development had been widely challenged at its first appearance, under Leo XIII his orthodoxy and his authority were recognized by the bestowal of the Cardinal's hat. The Council and the words of Paul VI have definitely established him not merely as acceptable but as the inspiring spirit of the Church's teaching of today.

Third, the Council has established freedom as the law of the Church. It is perhaps its most important practical achievement, and the most important task in the years to come will be to make sure that by eternal vigilance that priceless advantage is not again lost. An earlier chapter explained the special reasons that led the Church in the last century to champion the cause of a close relationship between Church and State and the special reasons that in modern times led the Americans and other bishops to call for a restatement of that teaching that gave a greater prominence to the importance of religious freedom. It was the Americans more than any others who considered it essential that there should go out from the Council a firm declaration to show that the Church did not grant freedom to persons of other religions with reluctance but recognized their absolute right before God to follow the dictates of their conscience. No one, said the Council, must be coerced into the acceptance of any religion—neither the Catholic nor any other.

To the Americans and the other bishops from outside Europe an assertion of the general right of religious liberty was essential for political reasons. Catholics in those countries could hardly expect to be accorded full religious freedom if they did not without equivocation concede full freedom to others. But the American bishops received the support of bishops from the North European countries who demanded on metaphysical grounds those freedoms that the Americans called for on political grounds. To the North Europeans it was essential to respect the personality of every man, and respect for his personality demanded full freedom to choose and practice his own faith. It was an assault on his personality to restrict his freedom or to force on him religious practices—even the practices of the Catholic religion. These two groups between them commanded a very substantial majority of the Assembly, and there was no doubt that the Declaration of Religious Liberty would be passed by an overwhelming majority if ever it came to the vote. But there were some South European bishops who were not yet reconciled to the abandonment of the Church's traditional reliance on State support. Those objectors had no chance of carrying a majority in the Assembly, but they had facilities for delaying matters and by inserting last-minute amendments were able to prevent a vote at the end of the third session. The result was that a number of the American bishops went home at the end of the session bitterly annoyed and that there were some articles in various newspapers in many countries suggesting that freedom was going to be betrayed by trickery. The pope, however, promised that the vote would be taken at the very beginning of the Fourth Session. This was done, and the decree was duly passed by an overwhelming majority.

It can fairly be proclaimed that the Council was a triumph for freedom. The Council has shown itself ready to allow greater freedom to the Catholic within the Church and unqualified rights of freedom to those who are not Catholics. But the Church is, of course, concerned not only with the religious practices of those outside the Church but also with the world in its secular aspect. The Christian religion is the religion of God who came down into this world. Promising the full reality of a future life, it yet cannot, like some other religions, dismiss this world as of no account. Insofar as it was true that the Church for some two hundred odd years from the Treaty of Westphalia in 1648 to the accession of Leo XIII in 1878 turned its back on the world and had little to say on its secular problems, it was in error. Since Leo's time it has fully recognized its duty to speak to the world on the problems of the world, and it was natural, therefore, that the Council should address itself to these problems.

As was argued in the analysis of the decree on the Relationship of the Church with the World, it would be idle to pretend that it had found a total solution for them. Indeed, while paying a tribute to Schema XIII, it might well be said that the Council did not really find anything very striking to say that had not already been said by Pope John in his two famous encyclicals and that by practical action Pope Paul by his visits to Jerusalem, to India, and to the United Nations has made a more striking impression than any that has been made by the Council. Those who clamour too unguardedly for decentralization should meditate on how much greater an impression is made on the imagination by a man than by a synod or a Council.

In general, to set against its many brave statements there are of course certain omissions from the Council's decrees. Some of those omissions—notably clear statements on birth control and mixed marriages—are simply due to the fact that these questions were taken out of the Council and into the pope's own hands. We are to expect new rulings by the pope about birth control in the near future. Whether they will satisfy everybody remains to be seen. But at least such decisions will not be decisions of the Council. The existing regulations about mixed marriages are by general consent the main practical grievance of non-Catholic Christians against the Church—the main obstacle to the growth of the true ecumenical spirit. The provisional rules of relaxation issued by the pope were, according to the frank statement of Archbishop Ramsey of Canterbury, insufficient to meet non-Catholic objections. Again it remains to be seen whether further relaxations will prove possible and, if so, satisfactory. But again such problems are outside the purview of the Council. Perhaps the two main omissions are those of any full consideration of the pastoral problems of the day—of the desirability or undesirability of the parish unit under modern conditions—and of any full statement of the fundamental faith such as would make the faithful able to distinguish clearly between what was of obligation and what was simply an ephemeral historical formulation. We have indeed the very important decree on the Constitution of the Church, but on this point it is not clear. In debates on birth control, on transubstantiation, and on other topics it has often not been easy to discover what was the exact status of the belief or practice that was being discussed.

The final verdict on the Council is, of course, that it is not the end but the beginning of a chapter. The Church, scattered over the world rather than concentrated in a few particular countries, is in the twentieth century in a situation different from any that it had ever previously occupied. With new inventions, greater rapidity of communications, new methods of production, the world of the twentieth century is a different place from any of its predecessors. A decreasing proportion of mankind is engaged in agriculture. Improved medicine has reduced infant mortality and created demographic problems. Inventions have brought mankind new comforts and luxuries and now threaten him with more terrible destruction. With the decline of national religions the old interdenominational antagonisms, which were as much the product of national rivalries as of religious differences, are no longer to be tolerated.

The first task of the Church is to recognize the fact of this new situation, and we can say that the Church under Pope John's leadership has, by and large, done this. Certain i's remain to be dotted and certain t's to be crossed, but the facts have in general been recognized. But of course all authority can do is to issue regulations, and the world cannot be saved merely by regulations. It may be wise to reform the liturgy, to enlarge the boundaries of freedom within the Church and our intercourse in charity with those outside it, to allow synods and decentralization and the like a wider expression of opinion. We can applaud the death of the Index. But these reforms do not of themselves introduce the spirit of Christ. They merely offer opportunities for its introduction. All turns on how the opportunities are used in the years to come.

SELECT BIBLIOGRAPHY

In this series: DVORNIK, FRANCIS: *The Ecumenical Councils;* D'ORMESSON, WLADIMIR: *The Papacy.*

ABBOT, W. M. (Editor): *Documents of Vatican II,* New York, Herder and Herder, 1966.

BAUM, GREGORY: *Teachings of the Second Vatican Council,* Westminster, Md., Newman, 1966.

BLANSHARD, PAUL: *Paul Blanshard on Vatican II,* Boston, Beacon Press, 1966.

KUNG, HANS: *Council, Reform, and Reunion,* New York, Sheed and Ward, 1962.

LEETHAM, CLAUDE, and CAMPION, C.: *Constitution on the Church: Vatican Council II,* Chicago, Fides, 1966.

RYNNE, XAVIER: *The Fourth Session,* New York, Farrar, Straus and Giroux, 1966; *Letters from Vatican City,* New York, Farrar, Straus and Giroux, 1963; *The Second Session,* New York, Farrar, Straus and Giroux, 1964; *The Third Session,* New York, Farrar, Straus and Giroux, 1965.

SHEPPARD, LANCELOT: *Blueprint for Worship,* Westminster, Md., Newman, 1964.

WILTGEN, RALPH M.: *The Rhine Flows into the Tiber: The Unknown Council,* New York, Hawthorn Books, 1967.

The Twentieth Century Encyclopedia of Catholicism

The number of each volume indicates its place in the over-all series and not the order of publication.

Titles are subject to change.